Travel
In the
Sixties

edited by

JOYCE RAGLAND

e-Book Press Publishing
an imprint of A & S Publishing
A & S Holmes, Inc

ISBN: 0692316876
ISBN-13: 978-0692316870
:

LIFE JOURNEY

Front cover art and back cover quote

The cover art for this book, "Life Journey," was originally created by Ann Ragland Bowns on silk using a combination of dyes and resists to form the complex design.

Ann Ragland Bowns' work encompasses a wide variety of media including oil, watercolor, acrylic, printmaking, batik, dye on silk, and sculpture. Ann's works have received numerous awards in juried shows. She is included in *The Best of Silk Painting* by North Light Books, Sunset Books *Crafts for Children*, and *Furoshiki Fabric Wraps* by C & T publishing. Ann taught at Sacramento City College, the American River College and in the adult education program in the San Juan school district. She gives workshops and demonstrations at High Hand Gallery, other locations, and at her studio. Please visit her web site to view more art at http://annragland.com

The poem on the back cover, "Life Journey," was written by Henri Frederic Amie,l, 19th century Swiss philosopher and poet.

"Life is short and we have not enough time for gladdening the hearts of those who travel the dark way with us.

O, be swift to love!

Make haste to be kind."

— Henri-Frédéric Amiel

TABLE OF CONTENTS

INTRODUCTION

Twenty-one writers and artists generously donated their talents to make this charity book project. The theme, "Travel in the Sixties," served as a general guide for creativity. Submissions reveal originality, brilliance, empathy, and use of humor as a saving grace for all of us who experience our own life's journey challenges.

The variety of pieces in this book are arranged in groups for each reader to use as a guide to the theme of each story or poem.

Proceeds from sales of paperback and e-books will benefit Alzheimer's patients, who have a most difficult journey in their final life's chapters.

Joyce Ragland, Editor
President, the Ella Ragland Art Charity

ON AGING, ALZHEIMER'S, AND A BUCKET LIST

From the Sixties to the Seventh Floor

Selene Castrovilla

The automatic doors open with a slight whir, and I walk in from the New York City winter. The Starbucks cups I'm toting have sloshed out many precious drops during the three block journey. I wonder how much coffee will be left for me and my Aunt Olga.

Tramping through this senior residence lobby, I pass several residents hovering like tragic Pac-Man ghosts.

At the desk, I ask admittance to the seventh floor.

The clerk uses the required elevator key. As long as I continually press the button the doors will open on my floor. The ascension is slow and rocky. The Starbucks carrier shakes; more coffee leaks.

My aunt, Olga Bloom, moved to this place only grudgingly. She didn't want to abandon her barge.

Decades ago she founded Bargemusic, a floating concert hall in Brooklyn. Gradually, she'd forsaken her bed at home for a lumpy but convenient couch on her vessel. She was afloat so much that she lost her "land legs," stumbling without movement beneath her feet.

At 89, she couldn't stay on board any longer. She'd fallen off the couch, breaking a rib. She moved here to the residence, planning to write a memoir with my help. But she stalled at the beginning, reciting the same anecdote every time we met.

I was frustrated, but not concerned. My aunt had always been odd.

In her, Alzheimer's took time to get noticed.

Then, suddenly, the sturdy Aunt Olga who could do anything was gone, replaced by this diminished soul.

Confused, she wanted to go home – to the barge.

When she set out to do so, pussy-footing to the curb and hailing a midnight cab to Brooklyn with no money in her pocket, her fate was sealed.

It was time for the seventh floor.

The doors open. Two residents are waiting, but the hallway aide tells them, "No, no. It's goin' up. Y'all gotta wait for the next one."

One of the residents snaps out, "You always say that."

The aide answers, "What can I say? I guess they gotta fix these elevators. They always goin' up!"

The resident huffs and heads into the activity room. I nod at the aide and follow the woman inside.

And there is my aunt – musician, scholar, groundbreaking visionary. Seated with several residents and another aide, she is playing Uno.

She used to have a Buddha-like serene smile. Now, she resembles a bewildered owl. She's wizened, but that's nothing new. Her skin was weathered by the outdoors long ago. But she's shrunken now, hunched into her own skin. Skinny like her skin is melting and all that's going to be left is bones.

It's her turn at the game, which no one except the aide beside her knows.

When informed, Aunt Olga is alarmed.

"Don't leave my side; I have no idea what I'm doing," Aunt Olga implores the aide.

"We're looking for a blue card, Olga." The aide's thick West Indies accent is warming. "Look! You got one! Throw it in!"

My aunt tosses the blue card to the pile.

The aide encourages the next player to participate. I move closer to Aunt Olga and smile.

She's blank for a moment when she looks at me. Then she says, "Oh, it's you!"

"It's me, Aunt Olga." I'm unsure that she really knows who I am. "What's going on?"

She frowns and scans the room.

"Do you want to come sit with me?" I ask.

She stands. Her chair scrapes the floor. "Let's get out of here."

We plod down the hallway. She's got her cane in her left hand and I take her other hand in mine. She pauses, gives me a long look, and I see her then - the real her, inside herself, glimmering.

She sees me, too. "Oh, Selene, I love you," she says.

"I love you, too, Aunt Olga," I tell her.

"Where are we?" she asks.

"We're at the place where you live now. We're going to sit and have some coffee." The weight of the carrier means there's enough left for us to enjoy, despite the splatter staining both cups and cardboard.

Her posture rises at the news. "Thank God!"

We trudge down the long hallway holding hands. It's a picturesque place. If I were going to be locked up someplace, this might not be that bad.

But of course it would be. Who wants to be locked up anywhere?

We reach the movie room. Four rows of easy chairs face a TV. On-screen, puppies frolic in a field. There's no sound.

We sit. Aunt Olga doesn't notice the puppies. I hand her a coffee. "With half and half," I say. Her favorite.

"Oh child, this is a godsend!" She opens the lid and sips.

She's happy for a moment.

Then she frowns. "I don't know what I'm doing," she says. She crunches the plastic lid inside her fist.

"Relax" I tell her. "Don't think about it."

This seems to work. She sips more, I yank off my layers. It's hot, though she's not sweating at all.

She pauses sipping and asks, "Where are we?"

"We're in the movie room, in the place where you live now."

"How did we get in here?"

"We walked down the hall." As an afterthought

I add, "We held hands."

"I held your hand through your crib spokes," she says.

"I know." She can't remember five minutes ago, but she remembers holding my hand in 1966 – which of course I don't. Our window of relativity is closing.

"You were afraid I'd leave when you went to sleep." I know, because she's told me this, too. "Your mother left you alone sometimes." This I know too well. She adds, "You gripped me."

"Thanks for staying with me," I say.

"Anything for you, dear heart."

There's a quiet. We're both drinking. Then she asks, "Where are you living now?"

Always, she asks this.

Always I answer, "In your house."

"My house on Long Island?"

"Yeah." She also doesn't remember that she sold her house in Brooklyn.

"Are you enjoying it?"

"Yeah." We go through this every time. "It's great."

"Do you think I could live there? I have to get out of here. I need to be alone. I just want to practice my fiddle in peace."

"Sure." I used to tell the truth, but I realized, what's the point? "We'll work it out. You can come."

"I won't be any trouble."

"I know."

"I can live in the little house in the back."

This is a new twist. "The shed?"

"It's got plenty of room."

"There's no bathroom," I say. Among other problems...

"We can build a tunnel to the house, so I can use the toilet in there, then go back out."

Even if I could overlook the impossibility of tunneling to the toilet, living in the shed would be absurd. There's no heat, there's no stove, even if she could be trusted to cook...I could go on.

"Fine," I say.

The thing is, even when she was well, she probably would've wanted to live in the shed. She's that kind of roughing it woman. A female Thoreau.

She says, "You fell off the dock."

"I did," I agree. I fell off her dock when I was two. We're back to the sixties again.

"Your mother and I were talking, and we turned our backs on you for a moment. You were gone."

"So I've heard." Thankfully that's one childhood trauma I don't remember, though she tells me about it all the time.

"You didn't make a sound. Not a cry, not a plop."

I shrug. I don't know why I silently slipped off the dock.

"We rushed to the float and looked down. You were sitting there in the mud, staring up at us."

"Thank God for low tide," I say.

"Indeed." She shifts in her chair. "I really want to come and garden. You think I can do that?"

Back to the present – her abbreviated version. "Sure."

"I won't get in your way."

"I know."

"I won't be any trouble, really."

"Right."

She leans forward and whispers conspiratorially, even though no one else is in the room.

"Selene, I don't know what I'm doing."

"It's okay. No one knows what they're doing," I assure her again. I give her hand a squeeze. "Just enjoy the moment."

She frowns.

On screen, the puppies prance. "What is this?" Aunt Olga asks, noticing the scene in front of us for the first time.

"Puppies," I say. "Dalmatians. Aren't they cute?"

"Why are they here?"

"I don't know. They just are. I guess they're a diversion."

"Oh," she says.

We talk about a few more things – like the novel I wrote based on our relationship and how she built the barge. She doesn't remember it, even though a copy sits in on her nightstand. I tell her about it. She's impressed. "Remarkable!" she declares. "Child, you are a wonder!"

I smile from the praise, but I also worry: if she forgot about the book, will she forget about me?

She'd read my manuscript when I wrote it, years ago.

We'd bonded through my story. We'd talked about issues I'd never dared broach before, and thus we'd reached our peace.

What does that amount to now?

We finish our coffee. Then an aide pokes her head in. It's time for dinner.

Visiting hours are over.

I lead Aunt Olga back down the corridor, her hand again in mine. Our feet make a faint treading sound on the carpet. "I love you," I tell her. My voice is frail. Leaving is the hardest part.

We reach the elevators. I ask the aide sitting there to please let me out. She sticks her key in the lock and pushes 'down.' There's a 'ding!' and the door opens.

Immediately, a woman with a walker tries to get on board.

"That one's going up, baby, you gotta wait," says the aide.

Aunt Olga doesn't question why I can get in when this woman can't. "Goodbye, dear heart," she tells me as we hug. "Come back and see me soon."

"Goodbye," I say.

I step in. She blows me a kiss as I wait for the door to close. "I love you, Aunt Olga," I tell her again. There's a panging in my chest, because she held my hand through those crib spokes, but I can't stay with her now.

Nor can I rescue her, the way she whisked me away in her battered Volkswagen Beetle for magical day trips she called "expeditions" when I was older.

My aunt gave me books; these days she can't focus on a page. She wholeheartedly tried passing her fierce love of music to me; yet she can't use her fiddle anymore.

She remembers just enough to know she's unhappy.

Maybe I don't want her to forget more, even if it brings relief.

I'm the biggest part of that more.

The elevator door creeps to the right.

Aunt Olga says nothing further. The door is closed.

Author's note:

This piece took place about a year before my Aunt Olga passed away. In those months she slipped even further into the abyss, and the last time I saw her she didn't know who I was. What a cruel end, to forget her accomplishments, all that made her happy – and the people she loved. What torture, to not be remembered by the person who nurtured me.

I miss you so much, Aunt Olga.

About the Author

Selene Castrovilla is an award-winning children's author and young adult novelist. One of her novels is based on her relationship with her aunt, Olga Bloom. Originally titled *Saved by the Music*, it has been re-released as *All Our Yesterdays*. Read more about Selene and her books at www.SeleneCastrovilla.com.

Only Sixty-eight!

Vicki D. Behl

Travel Journal, Wednesday, January 1, 2014

Happy New Year to my beautiful daughter and her beautiful daughter! Time to plan our next girls' road trip. Where will we go this year? What adventures will we chase and embrace? Some people think I'm too old to travel, but I'm only sixty-eight and I can't wait to see what adventures lay ahead with my favorite travel buddies, Laura and Jessie.

Love, Grandma Mary/Mom

It's cold here in Missouri and I'm looking forward to going somewhere warm. Maybe a beach. But, on the practical side, Jessie's in her junior year and is looking forward to college. This is our last year to check out some schools she might want to attend. Anybody know a warm place on a beach with a good university, where three generations can have fun together?

Love, Mom/Laura

Chasing and embracing adventures? Beaches?

Sounds great. I'm in! Only, can I bring Tyler? I'd miss him so much.

Love, Jessie

No!!!

Love Grandma and Mom

This was the beginning of planning our 2014 "girls only adventure." It's been our special tradition for my whole life. Grandma, Mom, and I take a trip, just us girls. We've been keeping this travel journal forever. It's all in a binder. The story of our journeys: the fun times, the scary times, and now the sad times, too. I feel lonely thinking that this year's trip was probably our last.

It snowed more in Missouri this year than any other year I can remember. Sure, we've had ice storms before, but this year, it was snow. Forget white Christmas. We had a whole white winter. With all the snow, I had a lot of days off school to help plan. Unfortunately, as we made plans and reservations through the month of January, we didn't realize then how the snow would keep coming and that I'd still be in school into June. Grandma reserved our first motel for the night of May 31.

The school was going to give me "unexcused" absences, which would have totally ruined my GPA and class rank. Mom had to go before the school board and argue. She ended up having to demonstrate the educational benefits of the trip.

Our itinerary called for visiting a couple of Natural Science museums and UT-The University of Texas in Austin. It was going to be a lot of walking and Mom worried that Grandma couldn't walk that much. I thought Grandma could do anything and she said she would enjoy it. "I'm only sixty-eight," she reminded us. So we set out on the last day of May.

Grandma wanted to drive first while she was still fresh and the first leg of our trip was the shortest. We stopped in Springfield, MO, about an hour from home, to visit the Missouri Institute of Natural Sciences. Grandma did fine all the way there, of course. After all, I thought, she's 'only sixty-eight.' It seemed like that had become her mantra.

Looking back, I think she was trying to convince herself that she wasn't getting old. She did forget things sometimes, like she'd call me by the wrong name once in a while, but all grandparents do that, don't they? Sometimes she seemed confused during a card game or something, but as loud as our family is, it is confusing. You can't always hear what everybody's saying. Anyway, she drove down to Springfield just fine.

We stayed at the Institute all morning and into the early afternoon. They have a volunteer program that I'm thinking about signing up for. I got all the information and forms while we were there. Mom thought it looked like a great opportunity. Grandma asked, "How will you get here?"

I thought that was kind of a weird question since I've been driving since I was fifteen and got my own car last year. She's ridden with me several times around town and I've been helping with the driving the last two years on our road trips together. I thought maybe she meant to ask where I'd get the gas money. I reminded her about my waitressing job. The pay isn't the best, but sometimes I get pretty good tips. It should be enough to get my gas plus a little extra. Maybe I can get Tyler to volunteer too and we can share gas expenses. It'll look good on my college apps and resume, too.

It was nearly two o'clock when we left and stomachs growled throughout the car. It sounded like a thunderstorm in there. Grandma drove again. There was a moment of confusion as we crossed the interstate on our way to the restaurant. The interchange there requires the north and south traffic to trade lanes as you go over the bridge. Everybody has to drive on the left side of the road instead of the right. It sounds crazy, but it actually works pretty smoothly. However, Grandma apparently hadn't ever been through that intersection before. I thought she was going to refuse to get over to the left and we were going to be toast, but at the last instant, Mom said, "Just follow the car in front of you." That seemed to help; we made it across.

We stopped for lunch in a home-style restaurant on the northwest side of town. We all got stuffed. Grandma wanted to take the first turn to tip. She laughed at herself when she had difficulty counting out the change. She told the waitress, "I'm not old. I'm only sixty-eight, but being on the road today seems to have me a little shook." Mom helped her figure out how much to leave and then we hit the road for Norman, Oklahoma.

Travel Journal, Saturday, May 31, 2014
We just got in from dinner in the charming

little restaurant next door. They had the old tablecloths that are red and white checkered. The waitress was real nice, but she talked kind of funny. I had a difficult time understanding what she said. Jessie and Laura can talk just like her and they've been making me laugh so hard my sides hurt. It's good to be out with the girls again.

-Grandma/Mom

Mom scared me half-to-death driving out of Springfield today. Finally, I told her to just follow the car in front of us and we made it through alive. The Institute in Springfield was fascinating. They had mammoth bones they found right there at the cave. They found the cave on September 11, 2001 when they were blasting for a road. Seems serendipitous that a blast in Missouri uncovered such a treasure the same day that there was such tragedy in New York.

-Mom/Laura

I hope I can go on a fossil dig with the Institute. They had a lot of fossils on display. I'd like to help put the puzzle together to learn more about primitive life. I was four years old when they discovered this cave.

Tomorrow we're going to the Sam Noble Museum of Natural History here in Norman. I can't believe all this cool stuff is so close to home! I'll have to see if Tyler can come down here with me sometime.

Looks like we're going to make a quick run to Walmart tonight. Grandma forgot her jammies.

-Jessie

The trip to Walmart was interesting, to say the

least. Mom took the lead in the store, as usual, with Grandma and me following. I stopped a moment to look at a shirt and when I turned back to where I thought Grandma was, she was gone. I must have looked mortified-that's how I felt. Mom had kept going toward the women's lingerie. I could see her several feet away, but Grandma was nowhere in sight.

A woman touched my arm. "I think you're looking for the lady who just turned toward the grocery department," she said, pointing. "She just got out of sight; if you walk fast you'll catch up."

Frantically, I headed in the direction the woman indicated, fumbling for my cell phone at the same time. I called Grandma's phone; she didn't answer. I called Mom's.

"What the heck are you doing? Where are you?" Her voice screeched in my ear. I could see her over in the clothing looking back where Grandma and I should've been.

"Look to your left. I'm by the groceries looking for Grandma. She just wandered off while I was looking at a shirt. Some woman saw her and pointed me in her direction, but she was already out of sight," I answered. I reached the aisle where I thought Grandma had turned, but she wasn't there.

"Stay where you are," Mom said. "I'll be right there." Mom was out of breath by the time she caught up to me.

We looked down the aisles on either side of the one I thought she'd gone down. No grandma, but we found a clerk stocking shelves. "Can I help you?" he asked.

"We're looking for my mother," Mom explained. "She's about five-foot-four, built like me."

"I think she might be the one that just asked where to find the PB and J," he said. He pointed us to the aisle he had directed her to.

We found her looking at the peanut butter. She had a jar of grape jelly in her hands.

"Mom, what are you doing? We were going to get you some PJs. Remember?"

I didn't give her time to answer Mom. "Grandma, I got scared. I stopped to look at that shirt and I turned around to say something to you, but you were gone," I said.

Grandma smiled at us and held up the jelly. "Land sakes, why are you scared?" Then she turned to Mom. "I found the PB and J." She sounded almost childlike.

"Why would we need PB and J?" I asked.

My mom took the jelly from Grandma and set it back on the shelf. "We don't need it. We came for pajamas."

"I came for PB and J, and I'm going to get it," Grandma argued and put peanut butter and jelly into the cart.

"Whoa," I said. "I guess we're getting PB and J tonight. Midnight snack, huh, Grandma?"

Mom gave up the fight. "I guess we'd better get some bread to put it on," she said, "and some plastic flatware, too. We'll have us a party at the motel tonight." We rounded up the food and went back to the women's lingerie. I had thought I would tease Grandma about getting something sexy, but now I just wanted to get out of the store. She chose something modest like you'd expect a grandma to wear.

I was never so happy to get back to a motel room in my life.

Travel Journal, Sunday, June 1, 2014

Laura drove today, so I got to sit in the back seat with Jessie. She talked and talked all the way to Waco-mostly about the museum and some boy named Tom or Tony. Oh, she says it's Tyler. I'm not sure what he had to do with anything anyway. The museum was fascinating. We got in an elevator and rode right up to a dinosaur's head. Not a real dinosaur of course, but the bones of it. It was huge. I think Jessie might be a dinosaur doctor someday.

-Grandma

Grandma, paleontology-the study of dinosaurs is interesting, but I really like living animals. The fossils are interesting because they show how we got to where we are. You know, like animals used to look like this, but now they've changed into something different. For instance, that six-foot long millipede we saw. Nowadays they're what, an inch-and-a-half, tops? If people had lived during the Paleozoic Era, how tall would we have been?

I knew we should have brought Tyler. He would've loved the museum. They had a cool skateboarding exhibit. I never knew skateboarding came from surfing. I got Tyler a little skateboard keychain. I got one for myself, too. Mine has Hawaiian flowers on it because that's where the sport originated. My skateboard keychain will be the only skateboard I'll ever use, but Tyler would live on a skateboard if he could. They also had a Samurai warrior's armor. Tyler's into that stuff, too. He likes to study martial art.

Mom drove today. Grandma sat in the back and talked with me all the way to Waco. We used to talk a lot, but since I've been so busy with school the last few years, we haven't had so much time together. Grandma just acts like those last few years haven't happened. "How old are you? Thirteen?" She's so funny. She's the greatest.

We had pizza for supper and then we stopped at a DQ for blizzards. Now I'm ready for shower and bed. After I call Tyler. I miss him so much.

-Jessie

It's been a long day for me, too. Especially since I did the driving. But tomorrow will be Jessie's turn at the wheel, as we head for Austin. We're going to tour the university there and then head down to Port Aransas where the school has a lab.

I have a funny story to tell on Mom today. When we got up to the desk at the museum to pay our admission, the clerk asked Mom, "One senior?" Her jaw dropped and she took a step back. She was so indignant. After an awkward moment, she sputtered out, "I'm only sixty-something. Uh, sixty-eight." Then she blushed like a school-girl and paid her senior's admission cost. She never wants to think about her age. I don't blame her. I used to think that sixty was old, but as I get more years tucked behind me, I realize sixty-something really isn't that old. And Mom just keeps trucking right along. She has a ton of energy. I hope I'm like that

when I'm sixty-something.
    -Laura/Mom

When we finally got to bed that night, I couldn't sleep. Grandma didn't think Mom's story was very funny. She looked confused first. Mom tried to explain what she thought was so funny about it and then Grandma just looked sad. Tears pooled up in her eyes and I thought she might cry. So I suggested we play Uno and eat peanut butter and jelly sandwiches before bed. That lightened the mood even though Grandma got confused when a bunch of word cards got played on top of each other. The "Reverse" cards especially got things mixed up. They get me mixed up, too.

I started thinking I should go over to Grandma's more often, like I used to. Maybe then she could remember that I'm not thirteen anymore. I tossed and turned half the night thinking about age-my age, Grandma's, my mother's. I wondered if sixty-eight was some magical age when you start forgetting important things about your grandkids or if it just happened because I didn't go see her often enough. Would Mom be like that when she turned sixty-eight? Was Grandma like this all of the time now, or just because we were on a road trip, exploring places we'd never been? My mind wouldn't stop asking questions and my eyes constantly visualized different scenarios playing out the possibilities of what Grandma must be going through at her age.

I had a funny thought. Do grandmas look at guys? Do they ever think a man is hot? I smiled, imagining my grandma checking out a man. Then I shivered. Funny thought, but creepy too. I hugged my pillow and drifted off.

Travel Journal, Monday, June 2, 2014

We started off this morning at Cameron Park in Waco. I could have spent all day there, unwinding and getting some exercise. We did a little hiking and sightseeing. There's a lookout place at the top of a bluff where you can look out and see forests and a river. Then there was a Lover's Leap. Seems like anywhere with hills has a "Lover's Leap." We ate a picnic lunch there, which we bought at a deli in a local grocery store. I climbed up "Jacob's Ladder," a weird zig-zaggy staircase, while Mom and Grandma waited for me at the bottom. Then we hit the road for Austin.

My turn to drive, so of course this was road construction day. It seemed to stretch clear from Waco to Austin. That was nerve-racking. I wanted Mom to take a turn driving, but she refused saying, "It's good experience for you. What if you go to school down here? You'll have to drive this by yourself to get home and come back." I have one word for you, Mom-airplane.

Anyway, now here we are in Austin. I'm nervous about the school tour tomorrow. It's so big here. Everything is big. Their waffles are even big. I didn't think I'd be able to eat the whole waffle I got at the motel this morning in Waco. I wish I hadn't. My stomach grumbled the rest of the day from trying to digest the thing.

-Jessie

Airplane, huh? I have one word for you, Miss Jessie-job. Better yet, why not choose a school closer to home?

I have to admit, I'm hoping Jessie won't like UT. It's just so far away. What if she needs me? It would take me two days to get down here. What if I need her?

On the other hand, I get excited for her just looking at the brochures about the campus and their science programs. It looks like a fun, cutting-edge place to learn. Jessie has high standards for herself. I don't think she'd be happy settling for a lukewarm school.

Since Jessie's new at driving in this kind of traffic, I rode shotgun for her. I felt bad leaving Mom in the back by herself, with no one to visit with. It's kind of hard for us to hear each other, talking from the front to the back of the car. It turned out okay, though. We listened to music all the way. We took turns listening to "our" music. Since Jessie was driving, we let her go first. She brought along One Republic. Mom brought the Righteous Brothers. That was a fun one to sing along with. I brought the Eagles. It was a good mix.

-Laura

I had the best time singing all the way down here today. Even little Jessie knows all the words to "Unchained Melody." I thought I did pretty well on "Hotel California," too, but now that new music that Jessie brought, I didn't know any of that. She sang solo on most of her CD. Laura sang along or hummed on some of it.

I don't understand why such a young person needs to visit a college. Jessie still needs to finish high school. She says she's interested in the school's lab down on the island near the ocean and it's a hard program to get into.

Now she's on her cell phone talking to that boy again. She's just trying to grow up too fast. I wish I could keep her young forever. And I'd be young forever, too.

-Grandma/Mom

I was so nervous about the campus tour the next day that I could hardly eat that night. What a way to spend vacation time. But I was nervous because I was so excited. I could hardly wait to get out into the world, leave that cozy little nest Mom and Dad had so diligently maintained my whole life. What better excuse to fly the coop? The words "Higher education" were almost like "Higher Power" in my family. And a career in Natural Sciences sounded good, too.

Not that home life was bad. We lived so close to Grandma, it was like we were one big happy family most of the time. She came to all my activities and we could go to her house about any time. And I loved our annual road trips.

This road trip had been different already though. There was a strange tension in the air, as if we were getting ready to turn a corner into a whole new world that none of us could be prepared for. We didn't know it was coming, but we should have. All of the road signs were there as we be-bopped our way down the highway, singing till our lungs hurt. I thought the college trip was the big life-changing event.

Travel Journal, Tuesday, June 3, 2014

Laura drove today. I think she was worried

that I'd get lost and confused in this big, new place. Give me some credit, girl! I'm only sixty-eight, and you're not that far behind me. Twenty years will fly by before you know it and there you'll be. Sixty-eight.

The college campus is huge. Almost as big as our home town, it seemed like, and we walked over the whole thing. My feet feel like oatmeal. I will be soaking in the tub as soon as Jessie gets out of there. She and Laura are going to go for another walk. Why anyone would want to walk more, I don't know.

-Mary

Why anyone would stay at the motel tonight when the beach is so close, I don't know. I will have to try to talk Grandma into coming with us. At least she could sit on the beach while Mom and I wade.

The school tour was great. Our guide was really friendly. By the time the tour was over, I felt like we were already good friends. She is actually from Iowa, so she's familiar with the road down through Missouri and Oklahoma. It gave us some common ground. The campus is huge, but the Natural Sciences are just on the opposite side of the block from where the freshman girls' dorm is. The buildings are beautiful. UT has an architecture program that helped design some of the buildings. And there are sprawling lawns. In one place there are these big old oak trees that have been standing there since the Civil War. I would love to come down here for school, but out-of-state tuition is horrendous. I don't know how I could ever afford it. They're going to send me some information on scholarships, though. That's my only hope. Good thing they didn't dock me back home for missing this week-thanks to Mom going down there and giving the school board an ear full.

-Jessie

Yeah, I really socked it to them, just like in Harper Valley PTA. Watch out for Momma in her mini-skirt.

My feet were tired after the campus tour too, but no way would I spend our first night down on the island cooped up in the motel. We're getting out there to enjoy ourselves-all of us-even if I have to drag Mom out.

-Mom/Laura

I noticed that Grandma signed out of the journal that night by her name, Mary, instead of Grandma/Mom. That's how she's signed out of our travel journal forever. I asked her about it and she says, "Why's that weird? That's who I am-Mary. I've been Mary for sixty-eight years."

I didn't argue the point. It's true after all. That's who she's been her whole life. She's only been my grandma for a fourth of her life.

We did drag her out that evening. "There's a beach here?" she said, as if she didn't already know that and we hadn't just driven over a bunch of bridges and then ridden a ferry. That's when I started really getting worried about Grandma. Mom reminded me that it had been a long day and we were all tired. Tired, yes. But Grandma, I realized, seemed to be in a whole different world. I think Mom knew it too, but she didn't want to worry me. Or maybe she was just in denial.

At any rate, we finally got Grandma to put on her walking shoes and go with us. We found her a comfortable spot under a beach umbrella to sit in the sand. She sank her toes in and then buried her feet in the sand. "Ah, home at last," she said, throwing her arms out and facing the ocean. She wore a closed-lip smile the size of Texas. I had tears in my eyes. For the first time, I thought I might actually lose my grandma some day. But really, I reminded myself, sixty-eight is not that old. We probably still had thirty more years together, at least. I could be a grandma by then. And she would come visit her great-grandbaby's child. We could have trips with five generations. That's what I told myself.

Travel Journal, Wednesday, June 4, 2010

Ah, today was much better. We sat in the sun on the beach, sipping cool drinks, watching the birds and the people. Laura and Jessie played in the water and walked along the shore, picking up shells. I had them go pick up a sand bucket for me so I could build a castle. It didn't look like much by the end of the day, but I don't care. It's all about the experience, I believe.

-Grandma/Mom

What a beautiful, rejuvenating day! We all got a little sun. Mom built a huge sand castle. Jessie and I picked up shells and explored the coast. Tomorrow we're going to check out UT's marine science center and maybe the estuary center. I'm not sure it's open yet. We'll also do some souvenir shopping, spend more time on the beach and check out the local food joints. This is the part of vacation

I came for.

    -Mom/Laura

    I had a great day too. But I see so many things that I want to know more about. I hope I get into UT so I can study down here. It would be fabulous. Of course, Tyler will have to come too. That might be the tricky part. His parents want him to go to a community college close to home so they can save on tuition and all that stuff. If he won't come, I'll just have to come down on my own. Grandma was right when we got to the beach last night. This is home.

    -Jessie

Some of the tension I had felt before seemed to melt away on the beach and washed away with the tide. I felt like a new person. I remember that I snuggled into bed by Grandma that night with a deep peace. I slept like a rock until the alarm went off.

It scared Grandma so badly, I thought she might wet the bed. After the initial shock of the alarm, we all pulled ourselves up and got dressed. We had PB & J sandwiches and then headed for the beach. The cool morning air caressed our faces and the first pinks and yellows of the morning reminded me of cotton candy. I could almost taste it. But it was a little salty.

Grandma seemed better after a day of R & R. Mom was the only one that seemed to still be a bit on the agitated side. She started in on the beach, rushing us along so we could get back in time to have a "real" breakfast at the motel and then get over to the Marine Science Center.

Travel Journal, Thursday, June 5, 2014

I finally talked Laura into leaving me on the beach while she took Jessie to the Marine Center this morning. Sakes alive! You'd think I'd never taken care of myself a day in my life the way that girl is doting over me. It's making me nervous, like she thinks I'm getting ready to drop dead or something. Are the vultures circling?

It was a lovely day to watch people. Speaking of people-oh my, was he good-looking! I'm talking about the tanned hunk with the beautiful dancing eyes who bought me a lemonade and sat in the shade of the umbrella with me. Maybe I'll move down here with Jessie.

-Grandma/Mom

Grandma! You're sixty-eight. Act your age. I'm seventeen and I'm not even looking at the guys here like that. Of course, I've got Tyler back home. I miss him so much.

The Marine Center is very cool-of course. We saw all kinds of plants and animals, birds, fish. I knew it would be awesome, but I wouldn't get to study down here until at least my junior year. I have to take all my general education courses first. They do a lot of graduate research here.

-Jessie

Oh yes, Jessie is so innocent. Ahem-I saw you eyeing our tour guide at the Marine Center. And I heard you asking plenty of questions you already knew answers to-like how soon you could start studying and researching at the Marine Center. Gawking was warranted. He was good-looking, but face it. No matter how hooked you are on Tyler, you're not blind. You'll always recognize a handsome feller when you see one. The question is, will you drool and follow each one of them around like a puppy dog? Some may be worth it. Others won't. Looks are not everything.

And then there's you, Mom! Checking out the guys on the beach. Between the two of you, I hardly have time to breathe on this vacation.

I need more beach time this evening. I can't believe we came all the way down here for the beach and it seems like I've hardly had time to enjoy it. Tomorrow we have to leave and head back for Missouri.

Love you, my travel companions!
Laura/Mom

I'll never forget how the beach sparkled in the sun that day. How the sea gulls swooped, their white bodies like exclamation points against the bright, cloudless sky. The warmth of the weather and the warmth inside me, of the love between my grandmother, mother and me. The love I shared with Tyler. Everything seemed so plain, so clear. Like there could never be doubts. No mistakes. The day is frozen in my mind, a still-frame in the middle of my life movie.

The next day, as Grandma drove us off the island (she had convinced Mom that after a couple of days there, she was familiar enough with the roads to drive), I rode shotgun with Grandma into a future that I never saw coming.

The other car ran a red light and T-boned us in the driver's side door. Thank goodness Mom was sitting in the middle of the backseat. She's the only one who didn't hit her head on anything. Besides being shook up, she was okay. I hit my head against my window, which shattered. Grandma took the brunt of the hit.

She screamed and screamed as she clawed at her seatbelt, trying to get out. I got out of my seatbelt and started trying to help Grandma. Mom said to stop and let the belt hold her in place until we got help. The other driver's front end was stuck in the side of our car and I could see that driver pinned back in the seat by her steering wheel, blood trickling down the side of her face. Mom called 911. I suddenly felt cold and like I might get sick. That's the last thing I remember for a while, though Mom says I talked to the EMTs as they loaded me into the ambulance.

I woke up in a hospital bed, with monitors beeping around me. Only slim shafts of light penetrated around curtains drawn closed. I heard feet moving by in the hallway and tried to turn to look, but pain in my head stopped me. I must have groaned or something. A woman came in.

"Hi. I'm Vanessa, your nurse. You've been in a car accident. Don't try to move just yet."

"Where's...?" I choked, remembering the accident all at once.

"Your mom is fine. She just walked down to the waiting room. I'll let her know you're awake." She hustled out before I could ask about Grandma.

I was in and out of a haze for a while in the ER. Fortunately, I didn't have any broken bones or serious head injuries. My head hurt a little and I had a bandage over my right ear where I got cut on the window. I learned that Grandma's door had to be cut open to get her out. Mom said she had a couple of broken ribs, a concussion and some torn tendons and ligaments in her shoulder. She was admitted to the hospital for monitoring overnight.

Dad and Tyler drove down, non-stop and got to the hospital late that night. We got a motel near the hospital. Grandma's car was totaled, of course. We'd all have to ride home in our car.

The next day we went back to the hospital. Tyler waited for us in the waiting room. Grandma was awake and waiting for her dismissal paperwork, but they still had her on pain meds, so she acted pretty loopy.

She didn't even seem to know us when we got there. She asked what time it was even though there was a clock right in front of her. And she kept picking at her blankets. She was doing this when the doctor visited midmorning. The doctor watched her for a moment, but didn't say anything about it. Just asked how she was feeling and if there was anybody else she wanted called. She asked for her husband.

Mom frowned. "Dad died six years ago, Mom."

"Not Dad," Grandma corrected. "He died along time ago. I want my husband, Johnny. Has he been called?"

Mom caught her breath. "I'll be glad when you're off these pain meds, Mom." The doctor caught Mom's attention and shook his head no.

Out loud he said, "Well, Mary. Other than a minor concussion and some shoulder problems, you appear to be okay. You'll need some therapy, at least to get the use of that shoulder again. Your doctor will need to have a look when the swelling goes down and see if maybe you need surgery.

"Laura, you're her daughter?" The doctor continued. Mom nodded yes. "Can I speak with you out in the hall, please?" Mom and Dad both went out with him. I sat by Grandma and held her hand.

"What are they talking about out there?" Grandma asked. "I wish they weren't tiptoeing around me, talking about me behind my back like I'm some old person."

"I know, Grandma. You're only sixty-eight," I said and started to laugh at her old line.

"Grandma? Sixty-eight?" she asked. "What?"

"You must have hit your head pretty hard if you don't even know you're my grandma," I said. "Or maybe it's the pain meds they've got you on."

"Pain meds?" Grandma asked, "What for?"

"You know, Grandma, for your head. You hurt it in the accident."

"What accident?"

The doctor told Mom he thought Grandma might have Alzheimer's and she needed to be checked out with her regular physician right away. He called her doctor, Dr. Louderback, and sent Grandma's records from the accident.

Mom cried first and then she started blaming it on the hospital and the pain medication. "That doctor doesn't know what he's talking about," she said. "He's got her so doped up right now, of course she doesn't know which way is up."

The swelling in Grandma's head was already down and the hospital released her to go home with us. Grandma acted like she didn't know who she was most of the time, much less me and Tyler. Tyler helped ease the situation with his jokes. He made her laugh and as long as she was laughing, she seemed all right. Even like her old self.

Dad drove to Waco and we stayed at the same hotel we'd stayed at on the way down to Austin.

"Mom, how about we go back to Cameron Park and get some exercise this evening before bedtime?" I asked.

"I'm tired and I think we'd better let Grandma get some rest too," she said. I looked at Mom and noticed things I'd never seen before. Like the streak of gray running through her hair and the two little wrinkles at the top of her nose, which seemed really deep because she kept frowning over dinner. Why hadn't I ever noticed these things before?

Tyler intervened. "What if Jesse and I go out for a while and let you all rest? Would that be okay?"

"Be back to the motel by nine," Mom said. She leaned against Dad like she was too tired to stand up on her own two feet. I felt like I did when I saw how quickly the flowers from my prom corsage wilted. Some things should be made to last longer. What was God thinking?

I barely got out the door before tears ran down my cheeks. "Come on," Tyler said and took my hand. I swallowed the painful knot in my throat and we walked out to the car.

"Are you okay?" Tyler asked. He opened the passenger side door for me to get in.

"I'm scared, Tyler. My mother's just forty-eight and my grandmother is sixty-eight. You see how exhausted my mom is? Like she doesn't have energy to hold her head up to eat or to smile at a funny joke. And Grandma-what's happened? A bump on the head, and she's outta here. I know Mom says it's the pain medication, but I was looking at our travel journal that we've kept every year as we go on vacations together. And it's like it's there, staring me in the face. Things I thought were funny along the way, really aren't funny at all. I'm losing my grandma, Tyler, and she's only sixty-eight."

"Hey, listen to yourself. She is only sixty-eight. You're not losing her yet or she would've died in the accident." He kissed the top of my head and shut my door. Then he walked around and slid in on the driver's side.

"Tyler, you're such an optimist, which is good, but I'm just not feeling it. Isn't Alzheimer's pretty serious? Don't they forget everything?"

"I'm not sure. I'm only seventeen and you're only seventeen. We have a lot of life ahead of us."

"I just always thought Grandma would be there for my life."

"She is here with you now. And they do have treatments for this, I'm sure. And whatever lies ahead, I bet what your Grandma needs most is for you to be strong. So buck up. Where's this park you were talking about?" I got out the map of Waco we'd used on our way down and located the park. It was a short drive from the motel.

We wandered hand-in-hand through the park until eight o'clock. "Let's get back to the motel," I said. "I'll feel better after a shower." Tyler drove again. It was nice to just sit back and let him take care of everything for the moment.

Yesterday we got up early at the motel and hit the road for home. Grandma seemed more herself. We listened to the music we each brought and sang along to pass the time. Then we played travel games like ZIP and the ABC game. Grandma laughed and sang and played along. I fell asleep on her shoulder at the Missouri line.

Finally we made it home late last night. Grandma's staying with us until we know she's going to be okay. Mom and Dad took her home this afternoon to pick up a few of her things. Tyler's going to come over for dinner with the family tonight. It's so quiet here now, and my mind won't stop whirling.

I've done some searching on the internet about Alzheimer's. People with Alzheimer's can live fifteen years or so after diagnosis. Maybe Grandma will get to meet her great-grandbaby someday, after-all. Probably not for another seven years or so, except that seems like forever. Maybe Grandma doesn't have Alzheimer's at all and it's just the pain meds, like Mom said. Then she could still live to see my grandbaby. She did seem a lot better yesterday and today, and besides, she's 'only sixty-eight.'

About the Author

Vicki Behl lives in the middle of twenty acres of woods near a rural town in southwest Missouri with her husband, their youngest son, two cats, three dogs, and more chickens than she ever wanted. She has been writing since she was six years old, when a local newspaper printed a piece she wrote in school about Columbus. Vicki stays very busy homeschooling her son, gardening, creating and teaching music, and writing. She is a charter member of the Lebanon Poets Society in Lebanon, MO and the Missouri State Poetry Society.

Sister Rock

Troy Garrison

During college and in my 40 years of teaching, I have had many aliases, each with a slightly different persona: Mr. G in Ava, Mr. Garrison in Nixa, Mr. Troy in Vietnam, Señor Troy in Costa Rica, Rock at S of O (School of the Ozarks), and Troy at Loretto Academy in Kansas City. One of my titles, in addition to student, actor, teacher, counselor, is a co-member of the Sisters of Loretto. The Sisters do not use the title, "Nun," they are called "members." One proud day for me, I became a co-member thus technically, I am an honorary nun.

At age sixty-something, I have a Bucket List.

To the Sisters of Loretto, I accredit my energy, enthusiasm and love of teaching. My most memorable years there, 1974-1979, were spent with Sr. Vicki Quatmann as our principal. Sister Vicki allowed her teachers to be as creative as her students. She created incredible memories and life lessons that we still use today. The Sisters of Loretto, the faculty and students all contributed to making us better students, parents, and citizens on the planet.*

In 2014, I want to continue the work Sr. Vicki started in the mountains of Bolivia. After leaving Kansas City, she dedicated her life to helping, as she described them, "the poorest of the poor." She taught a group of Bolivian Indian grandmothers how to knit. On trips to America, she sold those knitted hats and scarves, made of fine Alpaca wool. She took the money from hat sales back to the villages to enrich lives. For example, the hat money bought food, equipment and various supplies.

Sister Vicki did this work in Bolivia for many years. She died there doing what she loved. The villagers honored Sr. Vicki by painting a beautiful mural, a portrait of her overlooking the many villages she helped. It is painted on the side of a building that Sr. Vicki was instrumental in creating. They named the building "The Instituto Teccnologico Vicki Quatmann," and it houses classes to teach basic technology. To that I say, "Wow! What an incredible legacy!"

My plan is to go to Bolivia for the entire month of October, 2014 and continue Sr. Vicki's work to help make life a little better for the people of those villages. Sister Mary Peter Bruce, who lived in Bolivia for eighteen years and worked with many organizations to help the poor, is making this journey with me. She returned to the U.S. and represented the Sisters of Loretto as an NGO (Non-Governmental-Organization) at the United Nations. She will travel with me, interpret, and document our work in an ongoing blog. We aim to bring much-needed resources to those villages. The airfares and lodging expenses have been donated by a former Loretto student.

Sr. Vicki, you live on through your legacy of good works, and my Bucket List begins fulfillment.

*We've asked Loretto alumni to write down all-time favorite memories of teachers, float trips, plays and musicals, classes, Silver Dollar City, and various life-changing events. We will organize the anecdotes and send them to the Archives at the Motherhouse in Nerinx, Kentucky.

We've also put out a call for a small, medium, large, or extra-large donation to make this vision a reality. This is a tax-deductible donation, and for any donation over $100, I will send you a Bolivian alpaca scarf, hat or belt along with a photo of the villager who knitted it. For more information on how to donate, send email to tgarrison7@gmail.com. Thank you for participating, and I hope we can continue to spread the Loretto spirit.

About the Author

Troy Garrison holds a Bachelor of Arts degree. His career includes forty years as a teacher, counselor, and sometimes actor, salesman, and raconteur. He is proud to be an honorary co-member of the Sisters of Loretto.

interchange

Vicki Quatmann Honored on the Alto Plano Where She Died

HISTORICAL

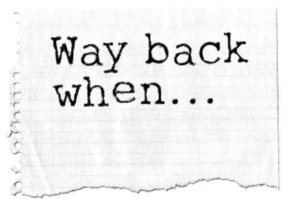

Route 66 Killed Grandpa Ragland

a true story

Joyce Ragland

The shadow of Grandpa Ragland's death hovered over my childhood. The shadow evolved into an event with logic, as I grew old enough to understand cause and effect. It wasn't a farm accident that killed Grandpa. He'd only run out of cornmeal.

Route 66 connected our family farm to church and town – a trinity of sorts. Our farm consisted of Grandpa Ragland's farm plus two more. After his WWII tour of duty, Dad bought out his sisters' shares in their family farm. A few years later, Dad bought two adjacent 80-acre farms, and with my mom, built one of the first modern dairy farms in post-war Missouri. Their modern operation and herd of registered Jerseys garnered feature coverage from *Hoard's Dairyman* and *The Missouri Ruralist.*

I experienced what some would call an idyllic childhood, but people who say that don't know the dangers we dodged on a daily basis. Farmers had a higher rate of injury than any other occupation except mining. Family gatherings focused on who said or did this or that –some pathos, much humor for balance—while we built our family folklore.

Talk included politics. More talk involved the weather. Small farm operations in the fifties and sixties did not allow for the luxury of irrigation or crop insurance. Letters from distantly located relatives got read and re-read. Remember when your Uncle Himself did this, and Aunt Whomever did that triggered more anecdotes.

Kids ate lunch inside with the adults, then got banished outside whatever the weather. We rotated our play through the yard, the smokehouse, the cellar— is the blacksnake down there?—and the barns. We dodged black widow spiders, rusty nails and dared each other to jump from the barn loft into a pile of hay below.

Sometimes we sneaked in to eavesdrop on the adults. We reveled in stories such as when Neighbor so and so got killed trying to brush hog big saplings. He should have known better. The ambulance driver said you could see his insides and him still alive. That poor man…

Highway 66 brought good, modern things to farm families and small towns with economic growth and tourist business. The highway brought ease of transport for emergencies. When the highway brought tragedy bad as any farm accident, the story was re-told many times at family gatherings over the years. Grandpa Arthur Hudson Ragland was the first person in our community to be killed by a Highway 66 vehicle. His death rocked the 1944 Southwest Missouri world.

Grandpa Ragland, even in his senior years, walked the mile or two from farm to town. He needed to save the aging work horse for farm use. Grandpa walked fast and with his head down. He is remembered as a daydreamer and a thinker. Maybe he was worrying about Grandma Mattie's treatments in Columbia's cancer hospital that day.

By the time of his last walk to town to buy cornmeal, he was hard of hearing but still had a shock of coal black hair on his head and vivid blue eyes. He likely had cataracts, too. He neither saw nor heard the vehicle until too late. Shock must have etched his face as he saw the vehicle bear down on him after he stepped onto the highway. The driver, too, would have registered shock and maybe yelled, "No!" as the man stepped into his lane. Grandpa's eyes probably widened with horror a heartbeat before impact. He bounced and fell still. The concrete of the highway was far, far harder than his Welsh-Irish skull.

The dangers of Route 66 grew exponentially over the next twenty years, as cars grew larger and faster. No seatbelts existed in the giant 1960s eight-cylinder beauties that rocketed down the highway at seventy-plus miles per hour. The cool driver held the right hand on the steering wheel and the left outside the rolled-down window. The super cool driver held the left hand on the wheel and the right hand around a girlfriend snuggled close enough he could smell her Breck shampoo.

Semi-tractor trailers carried tons and more tons of goods from town to town faster and cheaper than the railroads and each year more trucks filled the highway. The big trucks slowed on hills and vehicles had to pull into the oncoming lane to pass on the two-lane highway. Too many drivers tried to pass in too short a space, and often violated no-pass zones. Route 66 rolled with the curves and hills. Daring drivers tested fate—that a vehicle would not come over a hill head on. The curved concrete lip on the sides of two-lane Route 66 required a steady hand on the wheel because a nudge of that curb flipped a car fast as an eye blink.

By the time I-44 opened in 1962, the year I started high school and left childhood behind, the highway had been dubbed "Bloody 66." Grandpa Ragland's death paled in collective community memory by 1962 except in my family. At the Phillipsburg exit of I-44 even today, as I turn onto Old 66 toward my aunt's house, I think of Grandpa Ragland. The convoy of army trucks from Fort Leonard Wood passed and he thought the highway was clear, so stepped out and the milk truck...

Only an eyelash flutter in time, but an eternity in family folklore.

About the Author

Joyce Ragland holds BA Music, MA, EdS in Administration, and Ed.D., in curriculum. She is the author of more than one hundred academic publications in the form of books, articles, reports, conference proceedings, training modules, conference papers. She has been editor or reviewer of publications by Prentice-Hall, McGraw-Hill, Wiley, and other major publishers. In addition to academic publications, short stories, poetry, and two books have been published. She self-published one bilingual easy reader for a fund-raiser for her own charity that provides activities for Alzheimer's victims. Recent books published are *Dread the FRED*, a creative nonfiction book (November, 2013), and *Throwaway Child, the Life Story of John A. Garrison* (June, 2014) both published by Paperback Press. Read more of her work at http://JCRaglandWriting.blogspot.com and www.EllaRaglandArt.org.

Can I Help You, Friend?

Ellen Gray Massey

"I am Walking Owl of the Osages," the tall man said in his soft voice to the frightened couple clinging to each other on the steep muddy bank. "Don't be frightened, friends."

Just moments before while floating the Big Dry Wood River in western Missouri checking his traps, Walking Owl spotted their tracks. The lighter, smaller footprints were close to deeper irregular ones. Beside them were holes made by the end of a tree branch used as a cane.

Walking Owl paddled quietly to the center of the river as he scanned the area. He floated downstream around a bend before he saw the couple. His assessment from their tracks was correct. They were in trouble. In more ways than the man being crippled. A young pregnant woman was supporting the man who was covered with enough mud to disguise his race.

"Don't be frightened, friends," Walking Owl repeated. "Can I help you?"

The injured man glanced quickly at the woman

who whispered, "He's not after us."

The man nodded. Standing as erect as he could while leaning on his crude pole and favoring his right leg, he said, "We'd appreciate it, sir. We've lost our way."

"He hurt his leg when he fell back yonder." The woman pointed south up the river. "I think it's broken."

Walking Owl's concern and open manner convinced the man to trust him. "We are Joshua and Melody from Louisiana. We're on our way to Nebraska where we know some folks."

He didn't have to say they were run-away slaves. Walking Owl knew that when he first read their tracks. In this western Missouri county in 1857, the Missouri-Kansas border was overrun by Jayhawkers, Bushwhackers, and other outlaws from both Kansas and Missouri. Also run-away slaves from the South frequently fled through this area on their way to freedom in Iowa and Nebraska.

Walking Owl paddled his canoe under an overhanging tree where the bank leveled out a bit. "Get in, Joshua and Melody. I'll take you to a house I know where the people will see about your leg and help you on your way."

A few days later after Walking Owl sold his pelts in Ft. Scott, Kansas, and before he joined his fellow Osages to return to their home in northwest Kansas, he went back to the house on the underground railroad where he had left Joshua and Melody. He wanted to see how they were faring. Having heard rumors of Bushwhacker unrest along the border, he planned to help them get out of Missouri as soon as possible.

Before he left Joshua at the safe house, he noticed some horses in the barn. Perhaps Joshua might be able to ride the fifteen miles from the house to Ft. Scott, Kansas, where he would be safer from attack until he was well enough to continue his escape to Nebraska.

As usual he didn't travel the main road into Missouri. Since he knew the country since childhood when his tribe lived in and hunted the area before they moved to western Kansas, he hurried along back trails. Though no one saw him, he noticed there was unusual activity at a few houses. Men were gathering. From their angry mood, he suspected trouble.

At the home nearest the safe house, he got close enough to hear a few words. "At the McFarland place."

"Caught 'em this time."

He didn't linger to hear more. This was a lynching mob gathering. Somehow news of the run-a-way slaves had reached them.

He figured he could beat them to McFarlands by swimming his mare across the river. The men would take the longer way around the road to the ford. He slid his mare down the slick bank, swan her down the river to an inlet for a draw where the bank wasn't as steep. Once across, he flattened himself on his saddle and loped through the tall blue-stem prairie grass that almost hid his mare. Before he reached the barn, he dismounted and ground-tied her out of sight of the house. Behind a slight rise in the prairie, her bay color camouflaged her in the tall grass. On foot, without those in the house hearing him, he let himself in the cellar under the house.

Melody stifled a scream when she recognized Walking Owl. Feverish and weak, Joshua first raised up from his pallet, then recognizing the Osage, said in a faint voice, "Welcome, friend."

"Come, Joshua," Walking Owl said as he helped him stand up. "You must leave. There's a lynching mob on its way. Melody, go get the others."

"They's only Mister and Missus McFarland."

"Then get them. Hurry!"

Joshua was hot with fever. His leg was swollen, but using a cane, he tried to get up. With Walking Owl holding him, he managed to stand and hop up the few steps out of the cellar just as the McFarlands and Melody got there.

"You must all go," Walking Owl said to the group. "A lynching gang is on its way here."

Melody and Mrs. McFarland grabbed Joshua to keep him from falling.

"I'm all right, Melody," Joshua said. "Thanks, Mrs. McFarland."

"We've been expecting it," McFarland said. "Usually we send the people on quickly, but in this case with Joshua's leg and fever . . ."

"I've been doctoring him," Mrs. McFarland said, "but even the willow bark you suggested isn't keeping his fever down."

"We've got a place to hide," McFarland added waving his arm in a southern direction.

Walking Owl looked at the open prairie all around the farm buildings, "They'll find you here, no matter where you hide. Get your horses and I'll take you to Kansas on a back trail."

Even as the Osage was talking, from the west they heard distant hoof beats on the main road which ran about a quarter of a mile north of the McFarland place.

"Be quick," Walking Owl said. "Go to the barn and saddle horses for each of you. I've got my mare hidden. I'll help Joshua."

The McFarlands ran to the barn, but Melody continued to hold Joshua. "Go," Walking Owl ordered Melody. "Help them. Hurry!"

"Yes," Joshua said. "Go quick. I'm all right."

A line of trees and some outbuildings hid the southern cellar entrance from the approaching mob. Before the men reached the turnoff lane to the McFarland place, the couple and Melody were back with three saddled horses.

"This is all the horses we got," McFarland said. "I figured someone could ride with Joshua and help hold him."

Walking Owl nodded. "Come, Joshua, let's get you mounted here on Melody's horse. She's lighter and you can hold on to her."

"No," Joshua said. His strong, determined voice startled everyone. "I can't go. I'd hold the rest of you back."

Melody and the McFarlands all shook their heads. "We can't let you stay," McFarland said.

"Take Melody with you." Joshua looked at his pregnant wife. "I can't make it, but the three of you can."

"NO!" screamed Melody, clinging to her husband.

Joshua held her. "Go, so our baby will be born in freedom," he said.

"No, no!" Melody cried again. "I won't go without you."

"Think of the baby. They'll kill us all."

"We can't go without you!" McFarland said. "Come, man. We'll all get away."

"You won't make it with me holding you back," Joshua said. "Go!" He made an attempt to lift Melody onto her horse. Walking Owl stepped in and easily lifted her in the saddle and handed her the reins.

Mrs. McFarland said, "Melody dear, your baby. You must save him!"

The hoof beats on the main road sounded closer. By now they could hear men's voices but not distinguish individual words.

"Give me your gun," Joshua said to McFarland. "I'll hold them off until you all get clear."

Walking Owl held Melody in the saddle. When he was sure she would stay there, he turned to Joshua. "Come man," he said as he led Joshua to Melody's horse. Being a foot taller, he started to lift him up behind his wife. "Hold on to Melody. You can all get out."

In spite of his fever and incapacitated leg, Joshua held his ground. "We can't all make it. I'd hold everyone back. With a double load this gelding can't run fast enough and I don't know if I can hang on." From their position behind the farm buildings he couldn't see the advancing Bushwhackers, but the commotion they made said they were already on the lane to the house.

Joshua pulled away from Walking Owl and faced McFarland. "Give me your gun," he repeated. Without waiting for McFarland to hand the gun to him, he grabbed it out of his holster and stuck it in his belt. "We'll all be killed if I go with you. I'll hold them off long enough for all of you to get away."

With his cane he struck first Melody's horse on its rump and before Walking Owl could stop him, hit the other two horses. All three galloped toward the barn and the open prairie behind it.

McFarland yelled back, "There's more guns and ammunition in the gun cabinet."

"God bless you, Joshua," Mrs. McFarland said.

Melody sobbed. Unable to control her horse, but not taking her eyes off of Joshua, she held on to the saddle horn as her horse followed the other two in their mad rush to the river.

Joshua then hopped on his good leg to the front of the house. In sight of the Bushwhackers, he stumbled up the porch steps and entered. Protected by the walls, he squatted under a window and fired McFarland's gun.

Walking Owl watched the McFarlands and Melody gallop toward the river on the trail he had just used. From the river, still following the back roads, they could go safely to Ft. Scott where the McFarlands had friends on the next stop of their underground route.

It was too late to help Joshua, for his gunshot

directed the Bushwhackers' attention to him. Walking Owl hid nearby, his brown and tan clothing mingling with the vegetation.

All of the Bushwhackers zeroed in on the front of the house. "There's one of 'em," one yelled.

"In the house!" another shouted as he pulled out his gun and shot at the front door.

"We got 'em," the leader yelled in triumph. "Won't none of 'em git away this time."

The men behind him echoed their agreement. The shots that Joshua fired from the window slowed them down. A couple raced their horses across the front of the house and blasted the window. Joshua shot at random, not trying to hit anyone, but to keep their attention on him, and not notice the fleeing horses.

Next shots came from another window. Soon a couple blasts came from an upstairs window. Walking Owl wondered how with his bum leg and high fever that Joshua could move so quickly.

"They're all holed up here," one of the Bushwhackers yelled. "Y-e-e-haw!"

"Yeah, three guns, I reckon."

"There's no hurry," the leader shouted as he motioned to some men to surround the house. "They ain't goin' nowhere. We got 'em."

When one man dismounted and started toward the house, the ground in front of him erupted from Joshua's shot. The outlaw scurried back to his horse helped on his way by more gun shots in the ground behind him.

"Let's burn them out!" someone shouted.

Immediately one of the men lighted a torch.

Yelling and riding his horse back and forth in front of the house to reach the window where most of the shots came from, he tossed it on the wooden porch. At the same time another outlaw, galloping around back, tossed a torch at the back door, completely trapping Joshua in the house.

Walking Owl knew what the end would be. Unable to do anything and unwilling to witness it, he backed out of his hiding place. Before he disappeared behind the buildings over the slight swell in the prairie toward his mare, he glanced west. The three riders were almost to the river. Just before he was out of range of the house, he looked back at the farm buildings.

The front of the house was in flames. Joshua hobbled out of the back door where the fire hadn't spread over the whole area as it had in front. One of the many bullets fired by the Bushwhackers struck him in his good leg. The men were too busy watching the house to see the last of the three riders racing west across the prairie disappear in the timber along the river.

"There's one of 'em," someone yelled pointing to Joshua, who fell just outside the back door.

"Don't let him burn. Let's hang him," someone else shouted swinging an already prepared rope noose over his head like a cowboy ready to rope a steer.

"Yeah, Jake," someone yelled. "Let's get at it." All the riders whooped and joined Jake.

The leader dismounted and ran onto the back stoop, grabbed Joshua, and pulled him away from the burning house. "We got the nigger. All the others are burned up."

Jake tossed his rope over the biggest elm tree in the lawn. As the house burned, all the Bushwhackers gathered at the tree. They put the noose end of the rope around Joshua's neck and Jake jerked the free end, pulling the unconscious Joshua upright, his legs swaying back and forth.

Walking Owl knew he was dead even before the hanging. He fled to the river and waited there until everyone left and the embers from the house had cooled. In the light of the moon that night he cut the rope still holding Joshua's mutilated body in the elm tree and buried him in a level spot northwest of the house. So it would not be molested, he covered the grave with ashes and debris from the house to look like a natural result of the fire.

"You are the bravest man I've ever known," he said aloud when he finished. "Rest in peace."

About the Author

Ellen Gray Massey, BA, MA, has numerous articles, short stories, essays, and books published. In 1995 she was inducted into the Writers Hall of Fame of America and from 1973 to 1983 she directed high school students who published "Bittersweet, the Ozark Quarterly." Recent books are *The Bittersweet Ozarks at a Glance,* and novels, *The Burnt District, New Hope, Brothers, Blue and Gray, Her Enemies, Blue and Gray*, and *Footprints in the Ozarks: A Memoir*." Her writing has received numerous awards. Sadly, Ellen Gray Massey passed away July 13, 2014 at the age of 92. More about her incredible legacy can be found at http://www.ellengraymassey.com.

FOR CHILDREN

Riley's Curiosity

by Marilyn Smith

"I know Mom said not to cross the road," Riley the box turtle said to his brother, Roger, "but I want to see what is on the other side."

"Are you crazy?" Roger said. "Do you remember the time you talked me into going to the valley? You fell over a log and landed on your back, and it took all your strength to turn yourself over. Then a hawk tried to carry you away! I'm staying here."

"Bye," Riley said with confidence, although he was very frightened at the thought of going by himself. He slowly walked to the wooden fence, then crawled under it. Next, he needed to walk down into the ditch, and up the other side.

The hill was steep, and he was getting hungry. He decided to find a cricket or two. A few dandelion leaves sounded tasty, too. *While I'm here,* he thought, *I probably could dig down and find an earthworm. Oh, wow, lots of worms. Yummy, yummy!*

His full tummy was making him sleepy. After a

restful nap, he was awakened when the ground shook beneath him. He figured it was one of the semi-trucks his mother warned him about. He climbed the hill and onto the smooth blacktop surface. *Man, is this stuff hot. I've got to hurry before I cook my underside.*

The "rumble, rumble roar" of another semi made him hide inside his shell. *Whew, that nearly shook my insides out.*

Maybe, he was hoping, if he walked really fast he could make it across before another semi came along. "Oh, no, here comes a big black car. Why are you stopping? No, don't pick me up!" Riley yelled. His words never made it past the end of his nose, because it was tucked safely inside his shell with the rest of him. "No, don't put me back where I started. Now I'll have to start over."

He turned around and started walking again, and made it across the road, down the hill and out of the ditch. *Look at all that red clover. There is a lot more clover on this side of the road.*

The sun was starting to go down, so he decided to go home. Being gone after dark would worry his mother. If he could make it to the edge of the field, then it was only a short distance to the road.

"Put me down!" Riley shouted at the man who grabbed him. When he stuck his head out a wee bit, all he could see was a brand new, red, 1965 pickup truck. "Okay, you can put me down now!" Obey the man did, with a thud. He was dropped into a tall white bucket, to join four other turtles.

"How did you fellows get in here?" Riley asked.

"We were helping ourselves to some of Farmer McCarty's tomatoes and cantaloupes," the largest of the four answered. "Boy, was he mad!"

"I was crossing the road to go back home," Riley said.

The truck's movements and the squirming of the others were making him bounce all over. It almost made him turn over, which would have been scary.

Then the truck stopped, and the man dumped them into some tall grass. Riley wondered where they were? Which way was home? All the others cared about was finding someone's garden patch.

His instincts were telling him to walk toward the sun. He planned to steer clear of any road, for fear of another helpful motorist or a mad gardener delaying his journey.

He walked and walked, and was getting tired. Then he felt the grass moving. It was two children. "No, don't pick me up! Where are you taking me? I'm not a toy, I'm a turtle. I do not belong inside a house. No, don't put me in a box! Lettuce leaves? I really don't like lettuce leaves. Take me outside, so I can go home," Riley pleaded. "Kids! It's getting dark in here. Don't shut that lid. At least punch some air holes."

To his great relief, the kid's mother took him out. She even made them turn him loose. *Moms are so smart!*

Now, he had to figure out which direction to go. Since it was almost dark, he decided to make that decision the next morning.

The sun felt good. As soon as he could find a

lush patch of clover, he would eat breakfast, then head home.

If the sun was in front of him yesterday afternoon, it needed to be at his back that morning. Yes, heading away from the sun was the right decision, because he could see the double silos. The road was only a short distance away.

Across the ditch, up the hill and he would be on the road. *Why are so many people standing there? The parade -- I forgot about the parade they have every Fourth of July. Maybe if I hurry, I can get across before it starts. Hooray, I'm almost to the middle. A little farther and I will be on the other side. Too late, here comes the police car that leads the parade, followed by the school marching band. I'll hide in my shell and wait for them to pass.*

"That's some pretty fancy sidestepping you guys are doing," Riley told the students, but of course they couldn't hear him, their music was too loud. He then hoped he could cross before the floats and the horse drawn wagons started up the hill.

"Stop!" he heard a policeman yell. Then he heard his whistle. It was so loud, it nearly pierced Riley's eardrums. This brought the parade to a halt. The policeman picked Riley up, carried him to the side of the road and gently sat him down.

"Thanks, Mister," Riley said, hoping the policeman realized how grateful he was.

Riley walked down the bank, crawled under the wooden fence and made his way across to the flower bed. "Momma," he shouted, "I'm home."

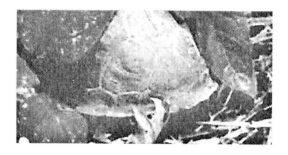

About the Author

Marilyn K. Smith has written a weekly column for the *Buffalo Reflex Newspaper*, called "A Tale or Two," since 1989. Over 2,000 of her articles have appeared in the *Reflex, The Ozarks Mountaineer, Springfield! Magazine, Senior Living Newspaper, Ozarks Watch, Springfield News-Leader,* and others. Anthologies her stories are featured in include *Cactus Country Vol. II, Golden Words, Echoes of the Ozarks Vol. VIII, Mysteries of the Ozarks Vol. III, Gifts of the Great Spirit Vol. II.* She serves as a contributing editor of the "Journal of the Ozarks" magazine. Her books include "A History of Highway 65, from the middle of the road," and "The Window Pane Inn and other short stories" published by Litho Press.

1960's Civil Rights

The 1964 Walk for Freedom in The Daily Tar Heel headlines
Old headlines from The Daily Tar Heel reveal the struggle for integration in Chapel Hill, a leader in the civil rights movement.

170 March Through Sleet And Rain

Board Vote Bypasses Accommodations Law

Mayor Of Chapel Hill: The Man In The Middle

Farmer Threatens Big Demonstrations

UNC Won't Push Town Integration

Jan. 14, 1964
About 170 black and white students marched 13 miles from Durham to Chapel Hill, showing support for an anti-discrimination law.

Jan. 14, 1964
The Chapel Hill Board of Aldermen voted down the anti-discrimination law by 4-2 at a meeting with more than 100 people in attendance.

Jan. 15, 1964
Civil rights leader James Farmer threatened to bring massive demonstrations to Chapel Hill if it did not desegregate by Feb. 1.

Jan. 16, 1964
Chapel Hill Mayor Sandy McClamroch set up a special committee to resolve the town's racial discrimination and segregation problems.

Feb. 4, 1964
UNC Chancellor William B. Aycock denied requests to use the University's economic power to speed integration in town businesses.

SOURCE: THE NORTH CAROLINA COLLECTION, THE WILSON LIBRARY

DTH/NAN COPELAND, MELISSA BORDEN

A Slice of Life in the 1960s

Vera Harrill

If the 1920s roared, the 1960s rocked, rumbled, and exploded.

In some ways it was the best of times and the worst of times. It was the most joyous and exciting in some ways; it was the most sorrowful and confusing in other ways. There were lots of positive changes and also much unrest and what seemed to be radical events.

Easy Rider, *Midnight Cowboy*, and *The Sound of Music* were popular at the movies. Credit cards appeared in wallets and purses; the Berlin Wall went up; Cassius Clay became Mohammed Ali; The Beatles invaded. An amazing thing happened in 1962 when John Glenn became the first astronaut to circle the earth three times and return safely.

Even more exceptional, in 1969 Apollo 11 and Apollo 12 astronauts landed on the surface of the moon. Neil Armstrong was the first to walk on the moon, saying, "That's one small step for man, one giant leap for mankind." Thus John F. Kennedy's dream of sending a man to the moon "in this decade" became a reality.

In our Midwestern, middle class, conservative family, things rolled merrily along.

My husband and I are both children of the Great Depression; we knew poverty but not much discrimination. We went to mostly all-white schools through high school. There was one Japanese family in my high school district. In my Baptist junior college, there was a light sprinkling of young people from other lands, but no African-Americans. This was also true of the state universities we attended.

After graduation Bill accepted a position with Sinclair Pipeline Company and we moved to Independence, Kansas, a small town in southeastern Kansas. We lived there during most of the 1960s.In the newsletter sent to Sinclair employees, there was a picture of Bill saying he was a new engineer for the company and also a picture of a black man saying he was a new janitor.

I remember the summer of 1962 as being one of the happiest times of my entire life. I had been doing at least two jobs for several years; I was homemaker, wife, mother, student, and teacher. My youth and abundant energy allowed me to bear and raise children, as well as hold a job outside the home. However, it was wonderful to have some of that responsibility lifted. Bill had a job that allowed us to take care of our needs, which were still very modest, and pay off the few debts we had acquired during the years Bill was in college.

The $160.00 he received monthly from the G.I.

Bill during college was a significant help in those day; plus we both worked either part time or full time. We don't remember the amount of salary he made in 1962, but we know it was less than $10,000 because I told a friend if we could make that amount it would take care of all of our needs and many of our wants. She said, "Well, you would need a little more than that." (My friend and her husband were making more than ten thousand.)

Independence, Kansas, was a small friendly town with many amenities. The children and I walked to Riverside Park almost every afternoon that first summer to swim in the pool. It was a good place to keep cool; we had no air conditioning yet and the temperatures often soared over the hundred degree mark. In the evenings our family could go there and ride the little train for one thin dime per person and the merry-go-round only cost five cents! There was a fountain that shot water high in the air and it was uplifting to watch the lights as they reflected on the dancing waters.

The Riverside Zoo was an added attraction and was set in surroundings as natural as possible. There were nice shelter houses for gatherings, play areas for children, fabulous storybook creations to admire and climb on. To me, from an impoverished background, it seemed a little piece of heaven. I was thin, tanned, relaxed, happy and full of energy that summer. It is one of the bright spots of light that always flash when I search for meaning in my life.

We occasionally saw people of color in the park, but none in the swimming pool.

When school started in the fall, the kids were

less than a block away from Riley Elementary School. Bruce, our oldest child, was eight years old and in the third grade; Joy was in first grade and learned to read that year; four-year-old Sherri, not to be outdone, learned to read along with her.

The schools in all the places that we lived had been officially integrated in the 1950s, but housing was still mostly segregated. The school our children attended was 99% Caucasian; the school where I would later teach was perhaps 15% African-American because of the location of the school.

In 1954, the Supreme Court had ruled that segregation in public schools was unconstitutional which overturned the "separate but equal" rules that existed in many states. Then, in 1955, the Supreme Court ordered that desegregation be carried out "with all deliberate speed." But it wasn't until 1969 the ruling that all schools be integrated "at once" that much action was taken.

In 1963, our youngest child, Sandra Sue - Sandy, was born; we decided four children was the perfect size for our family. Sandy was a fat little bundle and the doctor's advice, "Keep that baby cool," prompted the buying of our first air conditioner.

Thank God for air conditioning – it is much better that fanning with a piece of cardboard. People in poverty who can't afford air-conditioning still suffer in the heat.

There was a little neighborhood grocery store in easy walking distance of where we lived. It was a wonderful place for the children to go and buy small treats or pick up some item we needed. When my sister, Mildred, was staying with us the week after Sandy was born, she had a splitting headache so we sent Sherri to The Little Store, as we called it, to buy some headache medicine. Mildred wrote what she wanted on a piece of paper for Sherri to take, but we forgot to give her any money. When she came back she had the aspirin and the bill so we sent her back with the money. Sherri was barely five years old but she was well able to walk there and cross a fairly busy street and we had no worry about her safety or her ability to do whatever was asked of her. We are so thankful we raised our children at a time when it was safe for children to walk and ride bikes in their neighborhood.

There was only one Southern Baptist Church in Independence, and Bill started attending Wednesday evening services even before the rest of us moved to town. He was received with open arms – as were we all. There were other couples our age with children and we all fit right in. Here we had opportunity for service; we were needed and could make contributions. We could use our talents and our abilities to serve others. We also met challenges that helped us to grow spiritually and intellectually.

The only diversity we had was a lady from Germany who spoke with an accent. John Fitzgerald Kennedy was assassinated November 22, 1963, in Dallas, Texas. We all remember where we were when President Kennedy was killed. Sandy was a baby and I was at home with her; the three older kids came home from school for lunch; Bruce was fourth grade, Joy second grade and Sherri was in kindergarten. We heard on the television that

Kennedy had been shot in Dallas. We were all stunned. I remember Joy crying and saying, "He will probably die!" I said, "Well, maybe not." But he did die and the course of history took an unexpected turn. It was a devastating blow to our country. Many people, especially the younger generations, were so proud of our handsome young president and his family.

Neither Bill nor I had voted for Kennedy. Many of the Protestant churches were saying that electing a Catholic would be damaging to religious liberty. Sad to say, we believed that might be true. Fortunately the first two years of Kennedy's term of office had shown that was not so. Had he lived to run for a second term, we would have voted for him.

Two days later on a Sunday, Bill and Sandy were at home, the rest of us were at church when Jack Ruby killed Lee Harvey Oswald. Bill was holding Sandy and watching TV. "He shot him right in front of my eyes!" he said.

Martin Luther King, Jr. became a charismatic voice for the black people; his belief in nonviolence was met with police brutality and he was jailed several times as were his followers. Perhaps his most famous speech was given in August 1963 at the Lincoln Memorial in Washington, D. C.; the words stir us even now. The ending words say, "When we allow freedom to ring; when we let it ring from every village and every hamlet, from every state and every city, we will be able to speed up that day when all of God's children, black men and white men, Jews and Gentiles, Protestants and

Catholics, will be able to join hands and sing in the words of the old Negro spiritual, 'Free at last! Free at last! Thank God Almighty, we are free at last."

From that time forward on King's birthday, I would read that entire speech to my students even when I taught first graders. The ring of the words are melodic and inspiring.

It was in the 60s that black people started appearing on television and in movies more often in positive roles. It was a good thing, but even so it seemed very different, and some people had to adjust at first. For our family, life went on much as it had in the fifties, but we were aware of the stirring of great change in America. It just didn't impact us much.

Outside our safe circle however, things were starting to boil.

Short skirts came into style. Women were accustomed to wearing hose with a garter belt and longer skirts, so when skirts got shorter the undergarments would sometimes show! Mercy what a sight that was! Fortunately, panty hose soon came along to save the day!

A few women were starting to wear slacks when shopping and even to work. No one I knew had ever worn slacks to church. [I was the first woman to wear slacks to our Lebanon, Missouri, church - to a Wednesday evening Bible study and fellowship; I got disapproving looks from some other ladies – and this was in 1973!]

Independence had an annual celebration called Neewollah which is Halloween spelled backwards. It was a full week of fun activities. A Neewollah

Queen was chosen at a pageant in the stately Memorial Hall.

There was a street carnival, kiddy parade, and on Saturday a fabulous parade that drew bands, floats, and people from miles around. One year in the kiddy parade, Bruce, Joy, and Sherri went dressed as The Beverly Hillbillies; they rode bikes in one parade; another time, the girls rode stick horses wearing matching western costumes. The first time Sandy was in the parade, she wore a sombrero that was almost as big as she was.

No young black women were in the contest to be chosen for queen. A few black children were in the kiddy parade. There were very few Hispanics. In Junior High, Bruce's Spanish teacher was Mr. Diaz, a refugee from Cuba.

After the Civil War ended, laws had been passed to protect minority groups, primarily black people; unfortunately, many states found a way to ignore these laws or at least diminish their power. In 1964, a strong civil rights law was passed that banned discrimination because of a person's color, race, national origin, religion, or sex. This included a person's freedom to seek employment, vote, and use public places such as hotels, parks, and restaurants. It passed after a 75-day filibuster in the senate, and was signed by Lyndon B. Johnson who had become president after Kennedy was assassinated. Our part of Kansas was slow to embrace change. Black people were tolerated as long as they "kept in their place." One small town south of us had a highway sign saying, "All Negroes must be out of town before dark."

Many people had wider views, but not many were advocating for rapid change, including us.

The black people were in a hurry as indeed they should have been. For years many of them had low paying jobs and below standard housing. A black physician moved to town who received respect, but still some people didn't want him to live in their community for fear it would encourage more blacks to move there and take down property values.

During the happy years of the 1960s while our family enjoyed every advantage the town offered, blacks were not so fortunate. I don't remember seeing any black clerks in the stores or serving as waitresses. Our next door neighbor had a black maid who had worked for her in Oklahoma for years. There were black dishwashers, and garbage collectors. There were black laborers and a few who were self-employed. There were no black people in our church, but when we had a Vacation Bible School in our small mission church, several black girls attended. We welcomed them and applauded their courage, but there were some whites in the church who grumbled.

In our own little cocoon world of home, school, church we were insulated from a lot of unrest in the world. We were skeptical of some of the changes. It seemed change in some areas was coming too rapidly and in social areas seemed extreme. Free love? What was that all about? Hippies? Communes? Open marriage? Black Power with a fist? Burn the flag of the United States of America?

What did all the changes mean for us, our family, and our nation? Were we making progress or were we, as many people thought, in moral decline? How would all of this affect our children? There were more questions than answers. We approved of many of the changes, but we weren't sure what to think of some of them, and we didn't join in any of the campaigns for civil rights for people of color. We didn't even know how bad things were for them. We were about to find out, the news reports were full of stories of marches, repercussions, and police brutality. There were "sit-ins" as blacks tried to integrate restaurants. Freedom riders boarded buses bound for southern states knowing full well they could be met with hostility, beatings, jail, or even death. Still they "rode for freedom." It was a wild time.

Looking back from a wider viewpoint in my senior years, I have nothing but admiration for the brave pioneers who rode buses to the south and marched for freedom. How courageous they were to even enter a segregated restaurant and sit down.

Significant gains were made for civil rights, for people of color and for women, but it was not quick and it was not easy. Black people were beaten and imprisoned and murdered. It was a dark time for our country; a new day finally dawned, but it was a long time coming and was at great cost.

In April 1968, Memphis, Tennessee, the strong inspiring voice of Martin Luther King, Jr. was silenced. There followed a long period of mourning.

In 1967, when Sandy was four years old, I went back to work teaching library in an elementary school. When Dr. King was killed, I remember the sadness of some of the black students and unkind comments of some of the white adults. Our white janitor said, "Are they going to have a big funeral for all the hoodlums?" Hoodlums? I looked at him in disbelief.

One warm autumn day, a black boy who attended our school drowned in a gravel pit. He dived in the water and never came up. His classroom teacher and I attended the funeral; we were the only two white people in the packed church. This tragedy would not have happened had the boy been swimming in the public swimming pool.

June 1968 in Los Angeles, California, Robert Kennedy was assassinated as he campaigned for president.

When would this madness stop?

In 1969, Bill was offered a promotion in the company and we moved to Tulsa, Oklahoma. From there we went to Chicago, Illinois, back to Tulsa, then Los Angeles, California, and next was a longer move to Alaska, and after twelve years there we retired back to our farm in Missouri. During those years we were exposed to diversity of many kinds, and our world view was greatly extended – and we are thankful.

In 2014, when I watch news blurbs from the 1960s, I am appalled that I was not more aggressive in addressing some of these issues. I came slowly to the realization I should have been more involved.

Our time was coming that we would face discrimination; the '90s were our '60s so to speak as we had to deal with discrimination against gay people. We had close family and valued friends who were homosexual and we knew they were fine people and their sexual orientation was not a choice. Nevertheless, they were vilified and for safety's sake had to stay closeted – this is still true in our home town.

The 1990s was our time to lobby and march and write letters and get harassed. "We have come a long way, baby," as the song says, but we are still far from the finish line. As I write in 2014, our part of the country is in turmoil. In Ferguson, Missouri, a St. Louis suburb, an unarmed young black male was killed by a policeman causing riots and reactions that are seen around the country. The facts of this case are yet to be determined, and this confrontation is still under investigation. Prejudice is evident on both sides of the race issue.

Recently at a fast food establishment, I overheard a conversation which advocated killing people who were protesting. "If the police would shoot a few more that would settle them down."

Dear God in Heaven, is this 2014 or still 1964 – or 1864?

Many black people still live in poverty and lack educational skills for good paying jobs. In this area some people still use the "N" word – even in regard to the President of the United States.

Hate groups across the country sprouted like bad weeds after Obama was elected. Then when he was elected for a second term, an ultra-conservative branch of the Republican Party vowed to do all possible to see that he failed.

To summarize the 1960s, for me it was a blessed time. We enjoyed our four children, various cats, and a Beagle-mix named Skippy. Our family was young and we did not yet have the stress that comes as they hit the teen years, nor the financial challenge when they were old enough for college. We lived in a safe neighborhood with good schools. We were blessed by good neighbors and friends in our life. We were happy and busy in our church. We bought an older house that we loved and we were in the process of making improvements. Our careers were on target. Life was good.

Our world vision was challenged and expanded.

The 60s were a unique time in our country; somewhat of a great awakening. Too long had we slumbered while others suffered, and great strides were made in a few years. But fifty years later, we are still terribly prejudiced. Women don't make an equal wage. Gay men are murdered and lesbians beat up on a regular basis. De facto segregation keeps people of color in ghettos and then in prison. They need to be able to get a good education and a fulfilling job. They need hope. How slow we are to change!

But change is a constant and so we move on.

About the Author

Vera Harrill is a retired teacher, author and artist. She has published several articles and poems, as well as two volumes of family history and a cookbook. She is co-owner of the Lebanon Art Guild Gallery in downtown Lebanon, Missouri. She and husband, Bill, have four children and four grandsons. After retirement from their careers of teacher and engineer, they moved back to their farm in the Missouri Ozarks. Vera keeps busy with writing, painting, reading, and enjoying nature.

Topaz

Kay Gamblin

The precious kittens were so cute as they tried to get out of their box, jewel-like eyes were eager with anticipation.

Getting out of our box when young and eager to explore brought back memories. In 1964, after high school graduation, the world beckoned. College. There were many fences on the farm where I grew up. Riding my horse out on the back woods of government wilderness was out of my usual fenced-in pastures. But my trip to college proved to be not just getting out of fenced-in places, but into new realms of finding out others did not have the same kind of save, fenced-in world I had known.

On my first day at college, I met one of the most interesting, mysterious, and frustrating people of my college days. Topaz was a name interesting enough to begin with. Then, the mysterious facts of her life mesmerized me. She chose to tell about herself with much thought to each fact. Even her name was a mystery. Topaz simply refused to tell what her first name was. She said it went with her middle name, Topaz, but she hated it. We asked her for some clues to what it was, as girls do at night in dorms. She said it was two syllables. That is all she would say.

One day while studying her intently, I saw a blonde, golden-brown eyed young woman who was insecure with everything about herself. Being one to blurt out just about anything on my mind, I said, "Your eyes are like Smokey Topaz!" I looked at her.

She said, "If you ever tell anybody…"

I just couldn't understand her reluctance to be open about her name. She also told me she would never marry or have children, but would not tell me the reason.

A few weeks later, Topaz became very ill and was hospitalized. We heard she had a very serious blood disease and was receiving blood transfusions. Some kind of anemia. Her parents lived in the heart of Arkansas and were unable to visit her.

When she was twenty years old, her senior year in college, she told us her father was about eighty years old. That just seemed unfathomable. Then she told us her parents were not married. They just lived together and had several children.

I always joked about me being the blue-eyed, blond in a family with siblings who had brown eyes and hair. Topaz said sheepishly that she was the lightest one in her family.

One time when we were talking about books we liked, I told her about one that really enlightened me on how some people live. The book was, *I Passed for White*. Topaz wanted to know all about it and checked it out of the college library. She didn't think it told the whole story. Of course it didn't. It was the 1960s.

We graduated with our degrees, teaching certificates, and each had teaching contracts. The last time I heard from Topaz was a letter without a return address. She was teaching in Illinois, the land of Lincoln.

So many questions remain unanswered. In some ways, time can relax the fears of non-acceptance. Many questions remain. Was Topaz fighting the stigma of bi-racial parents? Was her serious blood condition a product of black heritage? After 46 years, I hope Topaz has found courage to face her torments.

About the Author

Kay Gamblin is a pseudonym for a college classmate friend of Topaz. Her dad was a teacher and taught Kay to always be a role model. She was raised on a farm where animals became a subject close to her heart. After college she taught junior high and senior high English and Remedial Reading. A career highlight was teaching GED classes for groups ranging from ages 16 through 70 years old. Names of people and locations in this story based on real events and real people, are changed to protect privacy.

Traveling Hard

Beverly Reid

Road-raging Sixties wheeled in,
rutting deep in our smug front yards.
Rocking, rumbling, they turned
this country wrong-side out,
uncovering its festering sores.
Their flags screamed protest, and.
Freedom, hitchhiking, finally got a ride.

Main street fire hoses fizzled,
couldn't water down
Black souls on fire,
or quench anarchy in Watts.
Draft card pyros and Dylan warned,
"…The order is rapidly fading…"
"… For the times they are a changin'."

Wheels screeched, ran bigots
off dangerous curves,
Vietnam sent us body bags,
hemlines, hairdos went up
leaving kitchens home alone, and

pot percolated peace in the air.
No one was seen on the grassy knoll.

Long-haired, wild-hearted
band-beaters drove us home
to wanting to "Hold our Hand."
Dance floor dust thickened the air,
slowly sifted down, settling
in our hair until it turned
silvery gray.

Shadows of the revolution
still ride around in low gear.
Daughters wear anything
they want to, and mine sings
with me and Neil Diamond
high in the bleachers, flicking
our lighters to "Coming to America."

About the Author

Beverly Reid writes to resurrect our life-groundings. Some of her stories are printed in "Echoes of the Ozarks" anthologies, and she has commentaries published in the Springfield News-Leader from time to time. She has a finished collection of short stories for some lucky publisher. Good fodder for her writing comes from these rich Ozarks hills of which she lays claim. Retirement has good days, and some not so good. She believes, "We live today from our memories. They are the essential essence of life. We must embrace them or our tomorrows mean nothing."

Hitchhiking Trip to New Orleans: Two Views

John R. (Jack) Rayl

It started in the hallway of the second floor in Ellis Hall on the Southwest Missouri State – SMS – campus in Springfield, Missouri. We were between classes in the Art Department and my friend Jack asked if I had plans for the semester break, which would be coming up in about a month, at the end of January. Jack and I had been friends since high school and he'd helped me get accepted in the SMS Art Department.

I said, "I really haven't thought about semester break."

Jack said, "Why don't we hitch to New Orleans and go gallery hopping?"

Jack was an experienced hitchhiker with many trips under his belt. I, on the other hand, had no hitchhiking experience. I said, "I have an aunt there and we could stay with her."

We went back to our separate classes and began, in our minds, to plan a hitchhiking trip to New Orleans.

As the days went by and we concentrated on semester finals, I asked questions about what to expect on our upcoming trip.

"We need to travel as light as we can, maybe take some food with us and try to find the best route, so we spend the shortest amount of time on the road as we have to," Jack said.

We were on the road the day after finals ended. Jack's mother drove us to the southern edge of town on Highway 65 and dropped us off. It didn't take long for us to get our first ride as a car with a couple of sorority girls Jack knew stopped. They recognized us as fraternity guys. We were dressed in typical college frat style. I wore green jeans, a dress shirt with button-down collar under a navy crew neck sweater and my TKE jacket. Jack wore khakis and a KA sweatshirt topped by a windbreaker. We both wore Ivy League haircuts, which some people called a JFK cut. We were both redheads. I had a mustache, the only facial hair allowed in the Marine Corps Reserves. I wore a black beret. Jack had a close-cropped beard.

The girls were going to their homes in Arkansas, so we headed south with them, the first leg of our trip to New Orleans. It was late in January and pretty cold, but not freezing and we were able to get rides in fits and starts. We got to Little Rock about midday, but didn't have any luck getting across the city going south. We decided to head east out of Little Rock, and then south.

We caught some rides and got to the little town of Stuttgart, Arkansas and came across an old rundown hotel. It was starting to get dark and the temperature colder, so we went into the hotel and got a room. The room was cheap and barely warm but there was an acceptable bed, which we shared. The Great Depression was still fairly recent history, and in our social class, sharing a bed with your brother or male friend was more common than it is now.

The next morning it was a little warmer but still chilly. We headed south on a road even less traveled than the one we had been on.

Jack taught me the ins and outs of hitchhiking. Never try to get a ride from someone as they are entering an intersection, but set up on the outgoing side so that the driver has a chance to see you, and always give them a place to stop at the side of the road. Look as non-threatening as possible. That was pretty easy, we thought, because we looked like regular college students. I carried a guitar, and Jack had a harmonica to entertain ourselves while we waited for rides.

"Never expect too much out of a ride, and always be respectful of even the shortest one," Jack added.

One of the interesting things that I observed of our ride givers was they never expected to see you again and if they had something to get off their chests, we were the perfect captured listeners. They gave us the local gossip, told us about their secret affairs, and who they were "gonna get" when they had the chance. We nodded and smiled and didn't butt in while they were venting.

As we got farther south, a traveling farm equipment salesman pulling a piece of machinery gave us a lift farther down into East Central Arkansas and across the Mississippi River at Greenville , into the Delta region of western Mississippi. He told us that if we were still on the road after he had called on his customer, he would take us farther south. He did.

Then things started to change.

Jack and I were twenty-two years old and, like all young men at that age, self-absorbed. We were mostly unaware of what had happened six months before during the Freedom Summer only a few hundred miles away from Springfield, Missouri in the states of Georgia, Alabama and Mississippi. The Freedom Riders and bus burnings seemed to be happening in some far off land and didn't concern us. We knew, as did everyone else in the country, that three young men had been murdered somewhere down south, but were vague as to just where it happened.

The previous summer, the Delta and most other rural regions of the south, had been flooded by groups of students, ministers, lawyers and others, perceived by the white population as Yankee trouble makers coming to change their society and class system. The black residents were not quite sure what these invaders' motives were. By the time Jack and I made our trip, white hitchhikers were not welcome.

We were blithely hitching through that area singing and waiting for our next ride.

We soon noticed we were not getting rides as quickly as we thought we should. And when we stopped at a gas station for a Coke we were greeted with, instead of, "Can I help you? Whadda *you* boys want?"

"Cokes," we said.

The clerk sullenly handed us the bottles and slapped our change on the counter. We grabbed the bottles, our change, and went out the door.

"Wonder what that was all about," I said.

"Beats me." Jack shrugged.

We walked on. We approached a small grocery store and through the half-opened door, saw a white woman walk toward us. We smiled, expecting to be greeted with some level of civility. But as we stepped closer, she slammed and locked the door in our faces

A little later, about fifty feet in front of a gas station/grocery store, we were waiting for a ride when a pickup truck approached. We stuck out our thumbs and tried to look friendly. The pickup slowed and we thought it was going to stop for us. It didn't. As it passed, a barrage of beer bottles came flying our way. None of them hit us but we knew we were in trouble.

Shattered brown glass scattered all around us. We looked at each other and one of us said, "We gotta get outta here."

But there was nowhere to go.

Within minutes, an old green pickup truck driven by a black man in his forties or fifties pulled over. He leaned over and called out to us, "Daes cummin to gets yuz boz, get inna truck."

Jack looked at me and asked, "What did he say?"

 Less than a year before, I had been training

with black Marines from the south and understood. "Get in the truck now, Jack." I kept my voice quiet, not wanting to panic him.

We threw our stuff in the back of the truck and jumped into the cab.

The driver sped away looking in his rearview mirror instead of at us. "Eys gonna take yuz boz otta hyre." He said some of the local toughs planned on gathering up a group and coming out to the highway and "whup" us.

Jack and I looked at each other but said nothing.

He drove us about thirty miles south to Belzoni and dropped us off. We said, "Thank you."

He said, "Yuz boz gotta git outta da delta," and drove away.

We tried to look inconspicuous and yet get a quick ride. A late model car with two white men in business suits pulled up. "They think you guys are COFO workers and we need to get you out of here," one said.

We had no idea what COFO workers were, but got into the back seat with our stuff and they sped away.

COFO, we found out, was an acronym for the Council of Federated Organizations. It seemed to me a somewhat misleading name for the various Civil Rights organizations working in the south to register black voters. The men in suits were Civil Rights lawyers from Detroit and Boston.

The lawyers told us that they had been threatened with bodily harm, had their tires slashed, and their car windows smashed. They could see we had no idea what we had gotten ourselves into. They drove us east, the fastest way out of the Delta, over the Yazoo River, through Yazoo City and up into the foothills where they thought we would be safer. They dropped us off at a roadside picnic area. We said our thank yous. They wished us good luck, turned around and drove back into the Delta.

We sat at a picnic table, got out our instruments started playing. Now cars honked at us, causing a Doppler effect as the sound of horns faded with the cars. It was just afternoon when a car pulled into the small parking lot at the picnic area. A young man got out who appeared to be two or three years older than Jack and me, and walked over to our table.

"Whadda y'all playing?" He asked.

I answered and began to pick and sing while Jack played the harmonica.

He sat and listened for a couple of songs and said he wished he had his guitar so he could join in. "Where ya goin?" He asked.

"New Orleans," I said.

"I'll give you a ride to Jackson."

"Great." We packed into his car and continued south.

He told us that he had the afternoon off and worked for the Highway Department. He'd heard there were two guys hitching through the area that might be "Folk Singers" or "Beatniks."

The term "Beatnik" was passé by that time and we were a little amused by its use. We would have answered to that label five or six years earlier. He asked us where we had come from. We told him of our quick trip through the Delta and the things that happened there.

"You fellows are lucky you didn't get hurt down there, standing on the roadside playing guitar and harmonica."

"I guess we almost did," I said.

In Jackson he asked us to stay in the car while he went inside his house. About twenty minutes later he emerged with a small duffel bag. He told us he'd called his uncle in New Orleans and made arrangements to stay a few days. He said he would drive us to New Orleans. He did.

On the way, we discussed his take on the Civil Rights movement. I suppose you would call him a southern moderate as he explained why the people in the south were so resentful of outsiders coming to teach the locals a new way of seeing racial questions. "We can solve this problem on our own without the help of outsiders. It might take longer, but *we* can do it," he concluded.

We arrived in New Orleans just before dark and he dropped us off at a service station. He gave us the phone number of his uncle, asked us to keep in touch, and said he would take us back to Jackson when we were ready.

I called my Aunt Marcelle, a Cajun lady, who was my grandmother's sister-in-law. "Hi Aunt Marcelle, its John Robert." I used my boyhood name. "My friend Jack and I have hitchhiked down from Springfield and wondered if we might stay a couple of days with you."

After a brief pause, she said, "Well John Robert, you can stay here, but your friend will have to find someplace else." I was flabbergasted. "Okay

Aunt Marcelle, goodbye." I don't know why she wouldn't let Jack stay at her house, because I never talked to her again.

"Well Jack, we're not staying with my aunt, so let's head down to the French Quarter."

It was about eight in the evening when we got to The Quarter. We walked around, probably looking like lost college students. We spotted a third-rate hotel and checked in. It was shabby but clean and didn't smell too bad. Again, Jack and I shared a bed.

The next morning we walked around the French Quarter. I had visited Aunt Marcelle eight years before, so I knew a little about what to look for. We went to the French Market, a pole barn-type building with an open air Café, to have coffee and beignets. It was much warmer than in Springfield so we sat outside, watched the people go by, planned what we were going to do that day. We would first go to all the galleries in the area, and see other things as we had time. I knew of the Cabildo, a French Colonial building that houses a Museum, Jackson Square and other tourist sites.

We walked around for a while, looked in windows, went in and out of tourists' shops, and looked over the shoulders of street artists. As art students, we were somewhat jaded in our view of their products.

A little after noon we started getting hungry and were thinking about where to go for lunch. We walked by Antoine's, a famous French Restaurant that we had read about and seen in movies and on TV. We looked at the menu posted at the door and decided to go inside. "Come in gentlemen and sit right here," a waiter in a French garçon outfit said in a slight, perhaps phony French accent.

Nobody brought us a menu but, instead, started bringing various courses of delicious French food. I don't remember what we had, but I do remember Jack and I got worried that we wouldn't be able to pay for it all. We were relieved to see that it wasn't going to break us and, what the hell, we're on An Adventure.

Later in the afternoon, we admired the work of a local painter in one of the higher class galleries. The painter had reproduced famous paintings with the principals wearing cutoffs, T-shirts, tennis shoes and baseball caps. We really liked his work. The proprietor said that if we waited a few minutes, we could meet the artist. We did.

The artist was George Dureau, a man of between 30 and 35. He wore a tightly trimmed, full beard and had on paint stained clothes. He looked like an eccentric artist. He seemed pleased that two provincial art students from some obscure Liberal Arts college in Missouri admired his work. We chatted, and after a while he invited us to his house for dinner. He gave us his address, the time to be there, and left.

The proprietor encouraged us to follow up on the offer to see the artist in action.

We went back to the hotel, showered, changed clothes, then sat and talked about what had happened to us in Mississippi.

By this time we had talked to quite a few people in New Orleans and had a better understanding of what had happened in the Delta. Jack and I realized we had, because of a concerned resident black man and a couple of unwelcome white intruders in Neshoba county, escaped serious trouble. We had hitchhiked close to Philadelphia, Mississippi where James Cheaney, Andrew Goodman, and Michael Schwerner had been murdered late in June the summer before.

When we got to George's house, we could smell food cooking. He invited us in. We wandered through his house, a classic French Quarter multi-family affair with fourteen-foot ceilings. We looked at finished paintings and works-in-progress.

George tabled the food, and although it was a simple meal, he made an exquisite presentation. Coming from a Midwestern meat and potatoes family, I was taken with the design and composition of each dish and plate. Each was a still life of color, form, and texture. It was my first exposure to Food as an Art Form, which has stayed with me throughout my life.

During the meal, we talked about form, design, balance, composition, texture, and other subjects that I now call Art Speak.

After drinking a couple of glasses of wine, some word clues and facial expressions, it dawned on me that the dinner was bait to entice two somewhat attractive young men to George's house to be hit on. Jack and I had been in the art, theatre, and music scene since high school so we were not surprised or shocked by George's advances.

George was on the cusp, at that time, of

becoming one of the more well-known New Orleans artists, and would have a forty-year career in the city He would influence the local art community and have national and international sales of his paintings and photographs. His last years were spent in a health care facility, where he succumbed to the complications of Alzheimer's disease.

I'm sure George realized that Jack and I weren't gay. We stayed as long as we thought polite, told George we'd had a tiring day and left his house.

We headed back to our hotel. We stopped from time to time to listen to jazz wafting through the streets from various bars and clubs.

We called our ride the next morning and found out he would be ready to leave the following day, and would come downtown to pick us up.

We spent that last day going to the Cabildo, walking on the river front, eating lunch at the French Market and returned to what we thought of as the best galleries. We'd had a full couple of days, so we decided to get back to the hotel early and rest up for our return trip to Springfield.

Our ride picked us up as promised, and we were on our way north. We told him of the various things we did and passed the time with idle chit chat. He took us to the northern suburbs of Jackson and dropped us off at a good hitching place. We said our farewells with, "When you come back next time, give me a call," and, "We really appreciate all the help you gave us." We all knew that Jack and I would never see him again.

We also knew that going back through the

Delta was a really bad idea, so we found a spot about thirty feet in front of the on-ramp to north I-55 to go straight up to Memphis.

Since the inception of the interstate highway system, it has been against federal law to hitchhike directly on the multi-lane highways. Therefore, it is not as easy to get rides on the interstates as it is on state highways. Getting to the best spot on the on-ramps was tricky. We got rides, but were slowed down by having to go from one off-ramp to the other on-ramp.

We got to Memphis late in the afternoon. We turned west and landed in West Memphis, Arkansas just before dark.

We caught a ride with a driver who was so drunk we almost got out of the car. He used obscure back roads. He weaved from side to side, and sometimes barely missed oncoming traffic. We finally made it to Paragould, Arkansas. Not where we wanted to be. We had planned to go through Jonesboro, Arkansas to Mammoth Springs, Missouri, then West Plains, Willow Springs, and on into Springfield.

The only place open in the middle of the night in Paragould was the Taxi Company. How a tiny little town like Paragould could have a taxi company was beyond Jack and me. They said we could stay in their "ready" room until morning. It was pretty cold now, and they had a hot stove in the middle of the room, so we were glad to be inside. We tried to sleep sitting on hard wooden chairs. Morning finally came.

We walked to the outskirts of town at the

junction of a north and a west highway. We thought that on a Saturday, we would have no trouble getting a ride. Not so.

By two in the afternoon, it was clear that we were not going to hitchhike out of Paragould, Arkansas. By now we were just about flat broke, so, what were we going to do? We walked back into town. Luckily, the bank was open, so I asked them to wire my bank in Springfield for a draft of enough money to buy bus tickets.

We left Paragould on the bus around five in the afternoon, and arrived in Springfield at midnight. Jack and I went our separate ways to our homes, woke up our folks and told them we were home. We would tell them the story of our trip to New Orleans after we had some sleep. We did.

* * * *

Over the years, Jack and I have talked about our trip to New Orleans and we've told the tale to many people. We are both amazed that nothing happened to us in the Delta during that turbulent time in our country's history. It was our youth and our naiveté that must have protected us.

I can't speak for Jack, but that five day hitchhiking trip changed me. I became more aware of what was happening in the country, and observed with better insight the escalating turmoil that followed in the next decade. I understood my own little world was not The World.

I personally never again went on a hitchhiking trip, and always did my research before any driving trip.

We are, at this writing, planning on driving a fifty-year anniversary re-visitation of that 1965 trip. In late January or early February of 2015, we are going to retrace our route as best as we can, and look forward to whatever adventures we will have. Except this time, we will drive my car.

About the Author

John R. (Jack) Rayl is a retired Commercial/Industrial designer. He considers himself an Existential abstract artist in the many media in which he works. He holds a BFA and an MFA in sculpture and also creates jewelry, various crafts and is a photographer. He has two daughters and two grandchildren. Writing is a hobby. He usually writes speculative fiction and a form of haiku called Senryu for his own amusement.

Hitching

Jack Bresee

Hitchhiking is a lost art in the USA today, impossible to practice. That wasn't always the case. At one time it was considered a normal and cheap way to get from one place to the other whether across town or across the country - especially during the war years. Picking up riders was nearly a patriotic duty.

Thumbing rides always entailed some inconvenience and danger but given the numbers involved, the dangers were exaggerated. High profile cases involving abductions and murders gave the impression that the danger was to the people offering the ride. But a greater danger was to the hitchhiker. Murder wasn't often the motorist's motive but one could never be sure if the driver was safe or at times, even a sober one.

My first lessons in hitchhiking came during my childhood days observing traffic on Route 66. The "Mother Road" ran directly in front of our home. My grandmother owned and ran a café, the proverbial Mother's Café and filling station immediately next door. I could see people standing at the driveway seeking rides. Hitchhiking looked easy—just stick your thumb out and a car would stop and pick you up. A little later my friends and I gave it a test run.

"The Highway" wasn't a place we were allowed to ride our bikes. When we wanted to take the mile or so trip to the square of our little town, we could thumb it and be there quicker and less tired than if we had ridden our bikes. We didn't realize that nearly everyone that picked us up knew our folks, which was the reason they gave us rides. Better for them to give us a ride than someone who didn't know us or care for our well-being. Many of our rides were in the back of pickup trucks and suited us well. A free ride with wind in our hair. The breeze ameliorated the scent of animal manure so often existing in the bed of the truck. The sight of travelers of little or no means – hobos - being fed at a picnic table provided by my grandmother behind her café assured me that somehow only good things could come to those who put their life in fate's hands. Life could be good to travelers.

Our next lessons in hitchhiking came from the Beat Generation writers, especially Jack Kerouac. His book, On The Road, was published in 1957. It was a manifesto of sorts. It served as a Hitchhiking Guide for Dummies although the Beats were slightly before our time. We were on the cusps of Beat & Hippie and very little had changed for anyone hoping to travel for free as far as conditions and circumstances for "bumming it."

Route #66 was The Mother Road and the

magic carpet for adventuresome young people. Also for those not so young, but they usually hopped a freight train, for various and sundry reasons. But hopping a train is an entirely separate genre and one I was involved in only twice. I would never have recommended it as a way to travel.**

The first rule of hitchhiking is, "Hitch" don't "Hike." One can trek all day or night for a meager gain of a couple of miles. The same distance can be traversed in minutes in a vehicle. It pays to wait for that ride that never seems to be coming because eventually, it will come. Sometimes you need to consider other options like a bus or even a taxi - but only in dire straits. The second rule is that your chances of getting a decent ride is to appear like you don't really need one. When Hitchhiking, cleanliness is next to godliness. If you look like a dirty bum, that will be the type person who stops for you. If they have a clean and comfortable car they won't want you to soil the fabric of the interior. Likewise if you are soaking wet, you won't get a ride so remember to bring a small umbrella. If it begins to pour down rain or sleet, the chances for getting a ride diminish in direct proportion to the amount falling. Do not bring a large stadium-sized umbrella. The wind from passing vehicles, especially semi-trailer trucks, can rip it out of your hands. An umbrella helps during light rain unless it begins to lightning, and then it becomes a lightning rod. This happened to my brother. He wasn't injured but it was a close call.

Some weather simply is not meant for hitchhiking, like downpours. If possible, seek out an overpass to get under. Find something for shelter. But snow can actually help. Traffic slows and the pitiful sight of a person exposed to the element can get a driver's attention and tug at a heart string - if it is a dry snow. Again, if you are soaking wet and caked with snow and ice, the edge is lost.

Third rule: Let people see you. Allow them to see they have nothing to fear. This is especially true with cops. Therefore, do not wear hats or sun glasses if possible. You have nothing to hide. Needless to say these are judgment calls. Anytime I was in the desert I wore a hat and sunglasses. Common sense.

Stay in well lighted places, not just at night. Standing in the sun vs. in the shade may seem arbitrary but it won't last for long if drivers like what they see. And don't sit down if you can stand. You will get all the sitting you like once you are picked up

Number four: Have proper identification and keep it handy in case someone asks for it, especially if that someone is a cop. A valid driver's license is essential.

The number five rule is being prepared to drive or talk. Most often drivers who pick up hitchhikers expect them to earn their keep by "spelling" them at the wheel or entertain them by regaling them with life history or other idle talk. It is in your best interest to help keep them awake and alert while they are driving. Often they want to sleep, so you drive and they rest.

Usually this comes after they get to know you a little. Once inside the car it is in your best interest to be accommodating. I have been told to get out in the middle of a desert because the driver grew tired of my company.

Last and most important, don't be afraid to be selective. Turn down the "lift" if anything doesn't fell right. If a gut feeling tells you to pass it up, then pass it up. It may seem that since you are asking for a ride, and they go to the trouble to stop, then you are obliged to accept it. Not so – especially if doing so might get you killed!

If the driver is drunk, pilled up, or if the ride will take you out of your way and off the beaten path, say, "No thank you." I once got stuck at a Pow Wow in Oklahoma and spent an entire day baking in the sunshine without a source of water because our host/driver was a Native American-costumed dance hobby enthusiast.

One should always be respectful. Especially to cops. But not only them, because you should always remember you are in a vulnerable position.*

All the negative experiences I encountered before our trip to New Orleans paled by comparison to what waited for John and me on that semester break once we left Arkansas and crossed over the state line into Mississippi and headed south. Drivers hurled beer bottles at us - some still full - and swerved off onto the shoulder trying to run over us. Verbal abuse was the least of our troubles. Store owners locked their doors before we could enter and the ubiquitous pickups sporting a Confederate flag with gun rack toting a weapon were plentiful.

To illustrate how stupid I was at that point I kept saying to John, "But we are white!" Hell, I was even wearing my Goldwater In '64 sweatshirt. I wanted to shout at them," Are you stupid? Can't you read?" Prudent fear stopped me.

The most scary part was when darkness closed in on us. All traffic disappeared from the highway where we were, first blacks, then everyone. We didn't even see one cop in the various small towns, not that we wanted to at that point. We had heard what Mississippi police were like. Jeeze. They were the ones who could legally pull the trigger. We simply got to a stoplight or street light and hoped for dawn. But we were saved before that time when a truck carrying several black men stopped and gave us a ride in the back of their truck on way to their work -before dawn, and from then on our luck changed for the better.

When our saviors in the truck let John and me out during our New Orleans trip, dawn was breaking. We thanked them for the ride and it was more than a perfunctory gesture. At that point in my young life there were precious few moments when I had truly felt gratitude. This was one of those moments. We both knew that we had nearly become victims of baleful ignorance and stupidity. We probably could have avoided it by being cautious and reading the papers or listening to network news before the trip. But that was not our wont. That didn't fit our image. Anyway, we both had reason to believe that our irons had been pulled out of the fire in the nick of time. It was great to have the guileless fortune of Voltaire's Candide. -not that either one of us truly appreciated it at the time.

The rides - good rides - started coming one

after the other. When we pulled into the metropolitan area of New Orleans, we began to see that we had run the gauntlet and survived.

We relaxed a little. There were still many obstacles to overcome but we were where we had intended to be when we started.

It was time for John to call his aunt in the suburb of New Orleans, Metairie, to line up a place to crash, to wash up and get some rest. We were exhausted, simply glad to be alive and not locked up. We were in Ville du Gras (Fat City). His aunt had invited him down at any time to visit and here we were. There were pay telephones everywhere in those days so he called her on one. That is when our plans went to hell on the spot in a new way. John's aunt told him that he was welcome but that bringing someone whom she had never met to spend a night under her roof was out of the question. He told her in not too subtle terms that if she wouldn't help both of us to forget it altogether. (John told me her name later became anathema in family circles.)

Once more good fortune smiled on us, for we found a cheap hotel room near the French Quarter and proceeded with our grand tour without having to be nice to a relative with a tendency toward punctiliousness. No place for a school chum, indeed!

We ate in nice places from Antoine's Restaurant to Tujacques on the quay and started each morning with bisquettes and cafe au lait in the old market area. We met fascinating strangers - one who invited us to his home for an elegant and authentic five-course meal with appropriate wines.

John even ran into a TKE frat brother in one restaurant.

But all the time, hanging over our heads like a pall, was the fact that we had to make the return trip home. I couldn't think about it without having my stomach tighten a little. Hitchhiking through Hell, as it were.

But we did make it out of New Orleans and to Paragould, Arkansas without major incident. The weather had turned cold and we spent our last night on the trip inside the dilapidated and tiny bus station. We shared space with three or four old men trying to stay warm while sleeping sitting up. The cast iron pot-bellied stove was cranked up and it danced a little on the floor, but it never really kept us warm.

Come morning, John wired his bank for bus fare money for the two of us and we were headed home and to our own warm beds.

Our trip to New Orleans was a life altering experience for me in many areas. Many of my viewpoints were turned upside down, most certainly regarding politics and the bulwark of Barry Goldwater's philosophy on State's Rights and the Tenth Article of the Bill of Rights. I knew then and I know now that some things, like Civil Rights issues, cannot be enforced without a strong federal government. Also, it dawned on me how provincial I was in my outlook toward other peoples in different areas of this nation and of the world. I learned that prejudice and hatred are color blind. Guilt by association is the bigot's world view. Reason has nothing to do with it. I learned that New

Orleans was not so much a southern city as an international one. That illustrated a fact that is true to this day. Rural areas around the world have more in common with rural areas of another nation than they do with metropolitan areas within their own national boundary. And vice versa. Marx may not have been the first person to point this fact out but nevertheless he wrote it also.

If the trip taught John and me anything about hitchhiking, it was that standing on the side of the road with your thumb out leaves you open to just about anything. So, the last lesson I learned about hitchhiking is this: Go from metro-area to metro-area and avoid the large patches of buncombe in between. Lucky for us, most people don't have malicious intent on their minds and the worst thing they do is treat you with benign indifference.

I have never stopped in Mississippi since that trip. I have flown over it, and that is as close as I've gotten. John and I are planning a return trip following the same path someday soon. Maybe we can determine if nostalgia is as good as it used to be. I doubt it.

*Sometimes cops do choose to mess with you, but mostly they have better things to do. They simply want to insure that you are passing through, and that any of their citizen charges are not molested by you. Let them know that you realize they are in charge. You show them ID and they run a check on you and let you move on with a warning that they have an eye on you. However, if you give them a smart-ass attitude they can find a million ways to mess with you including calling the next town or county constabulary to continue the process of harassment in their respective jurisdictions. They will even sit in their car just before the place you are standing and no motorist dares stop in view of the cop and pick you up.

On rare occasions a police presence even helps. It is in their best interest to not find their work load increased by strangers being injured or killed within their purview. There are all those reports to fill out and records to keep. Once in New York state I had a load of teens pull over as if to give me a ride, then as I approached the car at a run, they gunned it and left me covered in chat surrounded by a cloud of fumes and burnt rubber.

That happened more often than I like to remember. The only thing the hitchhiker can do is burn with impotent rage and follow them with a barrage of curses and obscenities. That is, usually. That time there happened to be a state trooper topping the hill just as they ripped out. He hit the lights and siren and pulled them over with great alacrity. Not only that, but I got a ride just then in spite of the cop being there. I took some sweet revenge as we passed the car full of smart-aleck kids.

Today the roads are designed and built not for humans but for automobiles and trucks. Stopping to pick up a person at today's high speeds means risking your life and the life of the person seeking a ride. Besides, stopping on interstate highways is universally illegal.

**Hopping freight trains: In deference to Woody Guthrie, Pete Seeger, John Hartford and all other folk singers who have glamorized Hobos and hopping trains, I am here to tell you it isn't so. Hopping freight trains is dirty and dangerous. It is also illegal, and rail road "Bulls" are private employees enforcing no trespassing restrictions on private property. A person bumming a ride has no civil rights per se, except those extended by ill-tempered private detectives. If you catch a ride, then they are responsible. Secondly, riding the rails does not refer to the rail road tracks, it means riding the rail on the under carriage beneath the cars on the struts connecting the equipment. They are next to the wheels. And if you lose your balance you're mincemeat. Just as important to the traveler, if you choose a companion while you are hitchhiking it is no big loss if you split up. Hitchhiking is like going out for coffee. Sharing a train with another hobo is like a long term commitment. In hitchhiking your buddy might get pissed at you, but the odds are he won't kill you for your shoes.

One doesn't get very dirty riding in an automobile or truck. No one has been dirty until they have ridden near a train's coal car for some distance. Last, the elements are brutal for the train rider. Consider the ambient temperature and conditions then, find the square of those numbers. Now you have some idea of what you will be encountering if you hop a train.

About the Author

Jack Bresee boasts of being a lifelong ne'ar do well, agitator, wannabe Socratic Gad Fly, and lover of languages. His first writing effort beyond school was a novel (unpublished) in the mode of Shirley Jackson and Stephen King, his favorite fiction authors. His favorite nonfiction writers are James Agee and Leon Trotsky. He soon became an inveterate and incorrigible writer of Letters To The Editor for several publications. First for The Militant, the newspaper for the Socialist Workers Party, then for newspapers in whichever city he lived He wrote articles for the Militants, most notably ones that covered strikes and working class issues. After being purged from the SWP in 1984, he wrote and cartooned for FIT/Bulletin in Defense of Marxism. During that period, he published articles for International Viewpoint, the print instrument of the Fourth International (Trotskyist). Today he is a writer/artist, a practicing curmudgeon, and a supporter of Latin American Liberation Theology. In spite of protest from many, he continues to write.

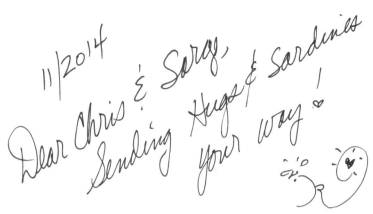

Mabel's Sardines & Apron Strings

Rosalie Lombardo

The civil rights riots in Chicago in the sixties were brutal. They penetrated every sense I had, including my sixth sense, the one that really commands attention.

Humboldt Park sits on Chicago's near northwest side. It covers 207-acres of beautiful green hills, walking paths, statues and huge trees. Living less than four miles away, it used to be our stomping ground on weekends. When the riots began, that formerly tranquil environment became a battleground between blacks, white and Hispanics.

We skirted around the Humboldt Park and south side areas of the city for fear of getting killed. Drive-by shootings were a common occurrence, as were having bottles, brick and molotov cocktails thrown at cars. It didn't matter if you were friend or foe, all that mattered was if your skin was white you got attacked. And if the perpetrators didn't have a gun to shoot at you, or something to throw at you and you happened to have been foolish enough to stop at a red light, your car got overturned by the sheer force of man power. It was ugly.

The news channels showed all the acts of destruction. On television it seemed surreal, but living just a few miles away made it particularly terrifying and left you wondering how much farther the riots would spread.

During the sixties many whites hated blacks and many blacks hated whites. The people were so invested in perpetuating their anger and hate that they had forgotten about the human spirit. Some people thought all skin colors except white were inferior. Some people thought, "Nothing wrong with 'colored' people; I just don't want them living next to me." Sometimes there are energies we can't explain about each other, yet they feel so familiar and loving. I was one of those few people who thought, "Why can't everyone recognize all people as human beings, no matter what skin color they have?"

In 1967, in the midst of the Chicago riots, I was fifteen years old and worked a summer job. I worked in a factory warehouse on the north side of Chicago on Roscoe Street, just east of Paulina Avenue. It was a huge white and red cinder block building with big blue windows and no air conditioning. Big fans in the building would blow you away if you walked directly in front of one, but they were so few you had to deliberately find one to walk past.

There was a seventy-one year old black lady with crooked stained teeth and semi-straightened cotton-looking hair. She had a wrinkled face, and kind, bloodshot eyes. She let me call her "Mom" even though I was a little white girl from a few blocks away, and she was an old black woman from the south side of the city.

Our shift started at 8:00 in the morning. She took three buses to come to work and she was always early. I, on the other hand, was always a few minutes late.

Every day at lunchtime, she'd stand in front of the same big fan, open a can of sardines, spread them on two slices of white bread with raw garlic and have her lunch washed down with one can of soda.

I liked to tease her by sneaking up behind her and untying her apron strings. When her apron fell off, she'd turn around and whine, with a Louisiana accent, "Baby Doll, I promise some day I'm gonna make you eat my sardines," and then she'd smile.

The smell of fish and garlic poured out of her sweaty skin all afternoon, especially after the building heated up to over 100 degrees. Yet, in spite of the uncomfortable sensory perceptions, there was a spark about her that made me smile. There was also a familiarity about her that went beyond smells or skin colors: the recognition of an old spirit who had a kind heart.

One day she brought an extra can of sardines with her to lunch, opened it and handed it to me along with a white plastic fork, and as promised, I did eat those sardines.

The only words she spoke were, "Make sure you return the fork to me." I stood with her in front of her favorite fan and together we each ate our respective can of sardines.

After lunch, I walked to the lady's bathroom and washed her fork. When I returned it to her, she held my hand for a moment and said, "How did you like them?"

"I liked them very much. Thank you, Mabel." I said.

She smiled and took her fork. I smiled back and returned to my assigned area. What she never knew, and I never told her, was that I had already liked sardines. My grandmother use to put them on a special spaghetti dish called "pasta al forno, "baked pasta."

In the midst of all that 1967 chaos and devastation, my senses had been touched in different way. I had been touched by a little old wrinkled black lady who still brings a smile to my heart whenever I think of her.

About the Author

Rosalie Lombardo is a member of the Springfield Writers' Guild, Sleuth's Ink, and The Society of Children's Book Writers and Illustrators She writes in various genres for a variety of audiences. Her works have been published in periodicals including The Kriya Flame, Fra Noi (Italian/American magazine), Spiritual Awakenings, Audubon Arrow, Ozarks Monthly, Senior Living, and the Bolivar Free Press.. In 2014, she was the recipient of "The Best of Springfield Writers' Guild" 20th Annual Literary Contest. She has taught a variety of classes at colleges in Missouri and

Illinois and through the private sector since 1996. She holds a B.A. with a major in psychology.

Birmingham (Travel to the 60s)

Bailey-Elizabeth Williams

Mama said the bomb wasn't meant for me.
I think it was meant for Pastor Martin 'cause he
be having them dreams.
Maybe those white men, maybe they didn't
know that we black girls be going to church too…
And we be folding our hands and praying,
taking communion just like their daughters do.

Maybe if I'd worn my church shoes,
the bad men would've never come for me.
I knew they matched my dress, but they always
just be hurtin' my feet.
I been thinking:
Did God christen the bombs that exploded my
flesh into sacrifice?
And do anybody be hearing those sacrificial
scriptures,
spoken in tongues, claiming Christ, before
everything went boom?
Before the smoke and the rubble baptized these
collapsing bones?

Maybe if they knew that we were like the most beautiful flowers, right before

wind and dust began playing tug-of-war with the delicates of our petals.

Mama said it only took one man to die for the sins of this entire world.

So how did that man let this church building tremble on my soul?

And I don't remember there being enough Holy Water to stop the smoke

or calm the burning.

I remember bones, crushed- too fine to ever be recycled into anything more.

Then no more.

Mama said some heartbreaks just be too hard to swallow at communion.

That some serpents just be findin' salvation in baptismal pools.

That some church mice just be screamin' America's dirty little secrets.

That some deaths just be too black and too white to be labeled holy.

That some sacrifice comes without permission.

That some sacrifice comes without fair warning.

That God can't always protect you from the Boogey Man.

So some baby girls will reach the pearly gates and she...

She won't be tall enough to turn the handle.

Mama said that some men will just be too
guilty to claim innocence with Christ.
But what did I do?
I never wanted to play with the white girls.
I never asked for integration.
All I wanted was a pair of roller skates,
maybe an extra piece of cake at dinner time.
Sometimes I just be thinking like,
like maybe God was too busy trying to protect
Martin to think about me.
I ain't never ask for his dream.
But mama, mama be saying that his dream just
been asking for me.

About the Author

Bailey-Elisabeth Williams authored
"Birmingham (Travel to the 60s)" while a senior at
Hazelwood West High School. In the fall of 2015
she will be heading to Dillard University to further
pursue her love of the English language. Bailey-
Elisabeth aspires to write fiction novels inspired by
real life events.

COMING OF AGE IN THE 1960S

Road Trip with Five Children

Toni Somers

"Are we there yet?"
Kids all whined.
"Not yet kiddos,"
Mom opined

"We just started,"
Barked the dad."
"Sounds like Dad
Is getting mad."

"How much longer?"
Evie queried
"One more question,
You'll be buried!"

"I'm so hungry,"
Begged wee Johnnie."
"Wahh-wahh-wahh,"
Wailed baby Bonnie

"Aarff-arf, bow-wow,"

Growled the pup,
When Russell ate her
Biscuits up.

Little Jimmie
Bawled again.
"Aren't we there yet?
When-when-when?"

Momma once more
Tore her hair
Mumbled, grumbled,
"Life ain't fair!"

"My sanity
Is on the skids.
No more road trips!
No more kids!"

About the Author

Toni Somers, grew up in Detroit, Michigan and has lived in New York, Maryland, Texas and Missouri. She currently resides in Springfield but has also lived in Columbia, MO.

She lives with John, her husband of 60 years and two miniature schnauzers. Her five grown children are scattered across the country---literally coast to coast from CA to CT as are her nine grandchildren. Toni began writing about 20 years ago upon her retirement as owner/photographer of a studio in Columbia. Her college degree is in studio art. She has also taught classical guitar and has worked at OTC as an adult education teacher. She still tutors students working on High School Equivalency certificates. Her writing interests are in short fiction, fictionalized memoirs, and poetry as well as a "maybe someday" novel. She has won writing awards in poetry and short prose both locally and nationally and has been published in two Chicken Soup For the Soul books, Life Lessons for Teachers, and Today's Woman.

Pristine Attitudes

Kay Gamblin

The Victorian Age may have ended in 1901 with the death of Queen Victoria, but many lives continued to be touched by the values of the earlier, pristine attitudes. Those of us who grew up in the 1950's and 1960's faced the new revolution of approaches to any references of sexual differences.

As a child, I scanned our newspapers and magazines of which many contained the most beautiful ad of a pretty lady looking into the distant horizon. Underneath the picture, was an ultra-feminine script which said, "Modess, because..." Being curious about its meaning, I asked my mother what the statement meant. Looking embarrassed, she said in a very hushed voice, "Pregnant." That did not seem logical, but knowing how my dad's family was when Mother was expecting her last child, 9 years after me, there was a grain of truth in that word. Even at that age, I knew the family tried to keep Mother hidden, away from knowing eyes in crowds.

As I drifted into adulthood, my mother's

knowledge of unfinished statements dealing with femininity was just a sign of her times, because...

Drivin' Draggin' and Dodgin' Police

a true tale

Marilyn Smith

The first Fair Grove, Missouri Blue Angels Car Club meeting took place September 26, 1960, with twenty boys attending - no girls allowed. We girls had to sit outside on car fenders, and patiently wait until the boys came out.

Country kids always drove as soon as they could reach the pedals, generally in fields and driveways. We had a large farm with lots of fields, and all those fields were dotted with rocks. On the days we didn't have other pressing duties, we were sent to the field to pick up rocks. I'm the youngest of five children and a bit spoiled, therefore I was given the easier jobs. On those rock picking days, I opted to pull the tractor up when it was time to move to a different spot. I guess that is when I developed my love for driving.

Driver's license and car registration checks were rare during those years, but when I was thirteen, in 1957, one of our county's finest had a roadblock set up on Highway 125, near Main Street, in Fair Grove, Missouri. I was tooling along at a fairly good clip, in my dad's pickup, when I noticed the flashing lights of the patrol car. I came to a stop, and waited my turn. As soon as the fellow in front of me was finished, I pulled forward. "May I see your license?"

"I don't have one." I went on to tell him that my dad was in the hospital, my mother was staying with him and I was on my way to the store to purchase groceries so I could fix supper for my two brothers.

"Okay, go buy your groceries, then take this truck home and park it!"

"I will," I assured him.

Our neighbor, James Turner, was next in line, and the officer asked him if what I said was true? James confirmed my story. No, I didn't lie about Daddy being in the hospital, but I did lie about going to the store to buy groceries. My trip to the store was for a bottle of pop.

My parents had a 1951 green Chevrolet sedan and a 1949 International pickup. I used every excuse in the world to get to drive those vehicles. Sunday was a time of rest at our house, with Mom and Daddy generally taking afternoon naps. My older brother and sister were married, and my other brothers were off doing their own thing. On one of those dull Sunday afternoons, I asked my dad if I could drive over to Evelyn's house? Her family's farm joined ours on the back, and getting to her house only required driving on a couple of old country roads. "I guess so, but don't go on the highway," I was told.

I dialed Evelyn's number, and it rang and rang. No one answered, but Daddy never knew that. While still listening to the ring, ring, ring, I pretended to make arrangements to visit my friend. In a short while I drove out our long driveway, making sure I headed toward Evelyn's house, then when I got to the corner I turned and drove to Minor's Cafe, located on the lightly traveled Highway 65, where all the kids hung out.

I obtained my driver's license the day I turned sixteen, Dec. 14, 1960. By this time, my parents had a 1958 Chevrolet, with an automatic transmission. I talked them out of that car as often as I could. It was one of those times that nearly got me into trouble.

It was a lazy Sunday afternoon, and I was allowed to drive to Minor's Cafe. I had no sooner arrived, when my brother, Jimmy, took over the car. A race was planned between him and some of the braver girls of the town. As usual, he won.

Following that race, a whole bunch of us decided to go to Joplin to see Steve, our new nephew. The car ran fine until we reached the edge of Joplin, then it started doing weird things. In a mile or so, the transmission went out.

We called my brother, Joe Wayne, and he came after us. Keep in mind, the car was my responsibility! I figured I would get into a heap of trouble, but Jimmy took the blame, thus saving my hide

My brother, Jerry Thomas, owned a 1961, black metallic Corvette. He said it ran much better after dark. Our brother, Jimmy, was the one who raced that car. Jerry's Corvette had glass pack mufflers that made a car rumble and roar. I loved that sound.

It was a ritual with me and most every other teenager in Fair Grove to drive south on Main Street, turn around on the square and come flying down that hill. If you let off the gas about half way down, with those glass packs open, Jerry's car roared and went "pop, pop, pop, pop, pop." I imagine the people who lived on that hill didn't get a wink of sleep until we all went home, but we never heard that anyone complained.

We went to drag races in Alton, Illinois two or three times, and Mo-Kan a few times. Illegal racing on straightaways around Fair Grove also took place; the long stretch in front of Minor's Cafe being a favorite. The races usually took place after 10:00 p.m., when traffic was almost nonexistent.

Drag racing on Glenstone, then Highway 65 through Springfield, took place also. The light turning green was the signal to take off! The drivers went through all three or four gears in a few seconds. Did I race my very hot, two door, hardtop, 1959 Chevrolet? You betcha. I won a great deal of the time, too.

My current car is a Prius. Taking off fast, then speeding along reduces our gas mileage. We're age sixty-something now, and more sensible, more frugal. Back in the *nineteen* sixties, we didn't worry about the cost of gas. Besides that, the Prius doesn't have glass pack muffler sounds.

The author, her future sister-in-law, and brother with his 'Vette.

About the Author

Marilyn K. Smith has written a weekly column for the *Buffalo Reflex Newspaper*, called "A Tale or Two," since 1989. Over 2,000 of her articles have appeared in the *Reflex, The Ozarks Mountaineer, Springfield! Magazine, Senior Living Newspaper, Ozarks Watch, Springfield News-Leader,* and others. Anthologies her stories are featured in include *Cactus Country Vol. II, Golden Words, Echoes of the Ozarks Vol. VIII, Mysteries of the Ozarks Vol. III, Gifts of the Great Spirit Vol. II.* She serves as a contributing editor of the "Journal of the Ozarks" magazine. Her books include "A History of

Highway 65, from the middle of the road," and "The Window Pane Inn and other short stories" published by Litho Press.

One Classy Lady

Toni Somers

"If I hear 'Mama, I'm hungry', or 'Mama, I need to potty', or 'Mama', anything, I'm getting out of this car and hitch-hiking the rest of the way. I kid you not, Jack!"

Interstate 70 through Kansas was never-ending. Traveling from Columbia, Missouri to Denver, Colorado in a 1963 Ford Falcon wagon with five children and an exuberant spaniel, I was living every mother's travel nightmare. What was the exact distance? Who remembered? Who cared? I'd given up.

When I turned my head to check on the kids, the odor of sour milk assailed my nostrils. Great! Baby Beth spits up her breakfast on the shoulder of my blouse, and I'm stuck in a hot car with sweaty kids, smelly clothes, and cheerful Jack. Life doesn't get much worse!

"It'll be OK, Hon. The kids are behaving better than usual. We'll stop for dinner soon. A break will do us good."

Why did he always read my mind? And why was he so damned good-natured? And how many times over the years had a nursing infant spit up on that same spot? Maybe 300 times? No. With five children, more than that. Possibly 500 times or even 1000? Who knew? It always smelled the same. They ought to bottle that smell to sell it to women who complain about empty nests.

I loved and treasured my kids. But let's face it. The trip had worn me out, burned me out. With a shaggy, straggly hairdo and armpits in desperate need of deodorant, I craved a shampoo and shower. Time was so short and preparations so hectic before the trip, I'd missed shaving my legs and armpits, trimming my toenails, and giving my neglected hair more than a quick brush. Forget time to buy a few new clothes for the trip.

"Honey, can you pick up my dry-cleaning by tomorrow? I need the brown suit for the trip."

"Mommy, Mrs. Bradshaw said you have to come to school to pick up my homework assignments for while we are gone."

"Mom, the laces on my Nike's are broken. I can't tie them anymore."

"Mom, I can't find my blue marble."

"Mama, doggie chew my blankie!"

"Wa-ah-ah-ah," wailed baby Beth in perfect harmony with all the others.

The chores proliferated. Then came a futile attempt to straighten the house so we wouldn't return to a child-created war zone. By departure time, every speck of my cherished free time disappeared.

Jack had surprised me a few weeks earlier.

"We need to get you away on a little vacation, Hon. My year as Chief Resident has been a tough one for us."

He ain't kidding, I'd thought to myself. Running the household and ferrying the kids and mowing the yard and all the other stuff coalesced into one gigantic job and the person who did it all was me!

Jack, the inveterate mind reader, responded.

"The Academy of Neurology annual conference in Denver is coming up in a few weeks. We'll make it a family vacation. You can have a relaxing get-a-way. O.K?"

"Sounds great, Jack. I'll have a serene and peaceful time with five kids in a motel while you're stuck in medical meetings. But what more have I got to lose," I'd said, slamming the oven door shut after shoving in a frozen pizza as I jiggled the baby on one hip and kept toddler Jim from eating more dog chow.

Ashamed of my thoughtless sarcasm, I blushed as Jack continued his gentle persuasion.

"I won't be in meetings all the time, Hon." He rubbed the back of my neck and the massage was as soothing as his words .

"I have a paper to present at one of the afternoon sessions, but then I can pick and choose. Not like my first year of residency when I apple-polished at every single event." He grinned at me.

"Those days are over. We'll be able to do some fun stuff with the kids. Maybe take a ride up into the Red Rocks. I loved collecting rocks there as a kid. And there's a great zoo there too. It'll be fun. I promise."

So here I was, three weeks later, in western Kansas wishing the drive were over and craving dinner and a chance to stretch my legs.

"Let's push on just a little farther, Hon," he said. "If we do, we'll have less distance to drive after dark."

Jack's request was reasonable, but I longed to escape the smell of sour milk, the sounds of the back seat brigade arguing, and the left-over-from-lunch taste of greasy fries.

"We're not doing fast food for dinner tonight, Hon." Jack had read my mind yet another time. "We're going to find a nice restaurant and have a leisurely sit-down meal. You deserve it, Hon."

How many times was he going to call me Hon? Guess he thought I was about to blow!

*****

As we walked into Neptune's, I recognized all the ingredients for impending disaster. Soft candlelight, linen tablecloths, string quartet, and a tuxedoed maitre d'. I looked down at my baggy, left-over-from-pregnancy slacks, and then at my stained and sour smelling blouse. I touched my hand to my hair. It felt even stringier than before and now it was sticky from road grime.

"A table for seven, sir?" Our host raised a

questioning eyebrow and straightened his already perfectly aligned French cuffs. "With a special chair for the little one?"

He looked down at our second youngest child, and so did I. Little Jim's runny nose had now crusted over. Yuck! I felt my face getting red.

"That'll be great," Jack responded. "We have a portable seat for our baby, but this little guy sure could use a booster chair."

Jack ruffled our toddler's hair. Great, I thought. Now Jim has messy hair along with a snotty nose!

"Doesn't this place look terrific, Hon? This'll be the ticket, alright. We'll have a quiet dinner. I can't believe we found a seafood restaurant for you out here in the middle of nowhere."

Jack had pulled out all the stops on his routine for soothing a frazzled wife. It began to work. As we settled our brood at a large table, I thought it might happen…a restful, peaceful, uneventful dinner. With five kids, I lusted after uneventful.

Jack was right. With a basket of breadsticks to tide the kids over and child-sized pizzas listed on the menu, peace seemed within reach. The Neptune appeared too good to be true. When I saw the Brook Trout Almondine on the menu I believed all things were possible! Faith is truly a wonderful thing I thought, as we ate our salads in relative silence.

My brook trout arrived at the same time SHE did.

"Wow. That's one classy lady," I heard Jack murmur.

I followed his gaze. The maitre d' preceded the classy lady and a distinguished-looking gentleman followed her. Jack was right. Gorgeous, well groomed, and regal, she graced Neptune's with her presence. I turned to watch her flowing movement across the room. The host seated the woman and her companion at a nearby table and then backed away murmuring he would return with a wine list. He had not asked if we wished to see the wine list. Looking at our menagerie, he probably felt it best we remain sober and alert.

She was not young, probably somewhere in her fifties, but stunning knows no age limit. The lady perused a menu, unaware of our glances in her direction. Graciousness and serenity surrounded her, and her entrance had attracted a number of more than casual glances. Her soft and elegant gray silk dress was devoid of sour milk stains. Her clothing hung like a dream on her tall, slender frame. Noticing her shoulder-length hair, as silky looking as her dress, I touched my own hair again. Nothing had changed. It still felt sticky. My pleasure at being eyeball-to-eyeball with the trout on my plate quickly dissipated as I visualized my own tacky appearance. Short, chubby (that was the polite term for it...dumpy was another option) and dressed in clothes that looked like garage sale rejects, I hoped the other patrons wouldn't notice the contrast.

At that moment little Beth woke up and squalled her hunger, my eldest daughter, Evelyn, whined that Johnny was kicking her under the table, Russell stuck his blue marble up his nose, and toddler Jim held up the edge of the table cloth while asking in a very loud voice, "What dis be,

Mommy?" My mortification increased as I envisioned heads turning toward us in disapproval. Surely, they probably thought, McDonalds or Taco Bell would be a more appropriate venue for us.

I would have continued to wallow in self-flagellation, but baby Beth made it clear she wanted her meal and she wanted it now! Retrieving her juice bottle from the bag and lifting her from the Infant-Seat, I cast a longing look at my trout. I had two choices. Feed the baby and eat another cold meal, or eat one handed, cradling her in the crook of my arm and holding the bottle in the same hand. This method of feeding, I am convinced to this day, is the first known cause of carpal tunnel syndrome.

Weighing my decision, I chose the beckoning trout even if it meant I had to eat it one-handed. The children and Jack dove into their meals in a rare silence while I struggled to feed the baby and myself simultaneously. I sensed movement nearby. SHE had risen and was bearing down our table. But surely, no one could object to our presence now. The baby was guzzling her bottle contentedly, the kicking under the table dispute had been resolved, and Jack had retrieved the blue marble from Russell's nose. Still she headed toward our table. Were we about to be banished from HER dining room and HER queenly court?

"What a beautiful family you have! They remind me of my own children when they were that age."

Her voice matched her demeanor, her words refreshing us like a gentle summer rain.

"You're so fortunate to have these big boys and

this lovely daughter to help you with the baby when you're traveling."

She smiled down at my brood, her eyes crinkling with pleasure. Skeptical, I looked at my children. They beamed with pride and sat up straighter in their chairs. Somehow, I knew that kicks under the table and attempts at nasal ingestion of marbles would diminish during the remainder of our meal.

"And now, please, may I give your baby her bottle while you finish your dinner? The trout is wonderful! You deserve to enjoy it while it's still hot."

She touched my shoulder kindly and, with equal care, took the baby from me. Beth stopped her eager slurping on the bottle to stare at this gracious lady for a long moment before beaming an angelic smile.

My family finished the meal on an island of calm tranquility. Each of us sat taller, felt more attractive, and spoke more gently to one another.

And the trout was perfection!

About the Author

Toni Somers, grew up in Detroit, Michigan and has lived in New York, Maryland, Texas and Missouri. She currently resides in Springfield but has also lived in Columbia, MO.

She lives with John, her husband of 60 years and two miniature schnauzers. Her five grown children are scattered across the country---literally coast to coast from CA to CT as are her nine grandchildren. Toni began writing in 1994 upon her retirement as owner/photographer of a studio in Columbia. Her college degree is in studio art. She has also taught classical guitar and has worked at OTC as an adult education teacher. She still tutors students working on High School Equivalency certificates. Her writing interests are in short fiction, fictionalized memoirs, and poetry as well as a "maybe someday" novel. She has won writing awards in poetry and short prose both locally and nationally and has been published in two Chicken Soup For the Soul books, Life Lessons for Teachers, and Today's Woman.

Crossing the Mississippi

Anita Lael

"I saw the Mississippi River. I crossed it." A small smile flitted across Kim's face as she read these words written by her seven-year-old self. Nothing like the autobiography of a second grader to take you back. Kim sat down on the porch and let her mind meander back many years to 1964. She reminisced about the road trip from Springfield, Missouri to Troy, Tennessee in the back of a 1963 Ford Fairlane 500. Red…

Watching at the door, Kimi waited impatiently. Finally! "Daddy's home!" She shrieked. Daddy had even taken off a couple of hours early for the trip.

"Give me a minute to change clothes, kids!" All three kids trailed behind him to the closet. Daddy's traveling outfit consisted of plaid shorts, a white v-neck t-shirt, and penny loafers.

Mama packed everything for the whole family packed into one suitcase that Daddy carried out to the car. "Let's go kids!" he called.

"Who has Heidi?" Mama asked.

Grown-up Kim fondly remembered the chubby little red dachshund of her childhood.

"Heidi, Heidi," three voices caroled as one.

"Here she is! Susan called, I've got her." *Mama held little James on her hip as she locked the house. The two girls raced to the car.*

"Kids in the backseat," Daddy directed. Kimi, the oldest sibling at seven, took charge. She drew two imaginary lines on the seat. "Susan, this is your space, baby James will be here in his seat, and I'll take the space behind Daddy. Everyone stay in their own spot and I'll hold Heidi," Kimi decreed as the red Ford hit the highway.

"No fair! Heidi is my dog," Susan whined.

"She's not your dog. She's all of ours," Kimi answered.

"You girls will take turn and share," Mama warned as she turned around to glare at them.

Kim, looking back, remembered sitting with her siblings in the back seat of the car. Baby James, at two, sat in a flimsy little car seat that offered little protection if any at all, and there were no seatbelts. Wow, it is amazing they were all still alive after growing up in the dangerous sixties, she mused.

It1964 was a much simpler time in many ways. Car televisions, video games, smart phones, iPads, and social networks were nonexistent. Mama passed a bag of books, crayons, coloring books, and an Etch-A-Sketch to the backseat for entertainment. Baby James soon dozed off. Kimi and Susan played *Who Can find the Letters of the Alphabet First?* on the highway billboards.

"Marlboro Man, M N O!" yelled seven year

old Kimi.

Thank God, there's no longer tobacco advertising on billboards, thought Kim, as she continued her journey down memory lane.

"I need to go to the bathroom right now, Susan called out, I need to go bad."

Daddy replied, "There's no place to stop now. We'll be at the best hamburger place in the world and will stop for supper in about an hour. You'll have to wait."

"I can't wait an hour," Susan moaned.

"Yes you can, Mama answered, Don't think about it. Look at a book."

Susan sniffled, "I'm going to pee my pants!"

"Young lady, we do not say the P word in this family, Mama scolded. I'll wash your mouth out with soap if I hear that again." And so the trip continued.

Joe's Burgers finally came in to sight and Daddy parked the red Ford in the shade. *"Let me get Susan to the bathroom", Mama said to Daddy, "You get the other two."*

Joe's Burgers, in the Missouri Bootheel, were the best hamburgers west of the Mississippi. Never was the trip to Tennessee made without a stop. The burgers dripped with juice, smelled like heaven, and were eaten on wooden picnic tables in the dusty parking lot under huge shade trees. Oh my goodness, they were delicious then, but Kim wouldn't dream of indulging in that many calories today!

Heidi was taken on short walk while Daddy ordered. "Here we go," He said and passed out a hot fragrant burger to everyone. Yummy! After the burgers he bought them twist ice cream cones for dessert. Mama and Daddy both smoked a cigarette before loading everyone back in the car.

"All aboard!" Daddy called out. "Ferry ride next!"

Crossing the Mississippi River on the ferry was the best part of the trip.

Pulling into the ferry stop, Daddy said, "Stay in the car until we're on the boat."

Kim remembered the sound of the creaking of the ferry boat ropes tied to the pilings as they waited. When enough cars were ready to cross, a loud low whistle blew and the ferry slowly eased out into the rolling muddy waters of the Mississippi River. Away from the dock, you could get out of the car and stand at the boat railing and look at the river. You could lean against the railing and feel the breeze and smell the pungent smell of the river. It was magical. Kim remembered being in awe of the enormity of the river! The water seemed to stretch on forever, but too soon, they reached the other side and the red Ford once again hit the highway.

"Kids it will be late when we get in. Try to get some sleep. It will make the time go faster." Mama said. Mama took baby James on her lap, another dangerous act of the past, while Kimi and Susan tried to lie down on the backseat.

"Kimi has her feet on me!" Susan complained.

Mama warned, "Don't make me turn around there, girls."

Kim got up for a glass of wine then returned to the porch and let the memory of the low voices of

Mama and Daddy, the soft music from the radio, and the rhythmic hum of the tires as the journey continued envelop her. When had she ever again felt that safe and cared for as she had in that car with her family on those long ago trips to Tennessee?

She remembered arriving at the Tennessee relatives late in the night. Daddy would pull in the drive and their posse of blue tick hounds would come to sniff Heidi and lead them inside. The relatives would be drinking coffee, eating popcorn, maybe playing cards, and so happy to welcome them. Mama and Daddy would carry sleeping kids to pallets on the floor and they would sleep soundly and peacefully until morning.

About the Author

Dr. Anita Lael holds the rank of Associate Professor in the Department of Education at Lincoln University in Jefferson City. Anita serves on the Missouri Department of Elementary and Secondary Education Literacy Advisory Committee. She is a former public school teacher, principal, teacher trainer for the Missouri Reading Initiative, and adjunct instructor at Drury University. Anita is married to Steven, has a daughter, Stephanie Lewis, a son-in-law Tony, and a chocolate lab named Woodley. Anita teaches yoga at Sumits Hot Yoga in Springfield and Wilson's Yoga in Jefferson City.

Chasing Girls

by Ken Williams

In 1965 I was a college student. I lived at Point Lookout, Mo. The blessed week-end arrived and I signed out for the week-end as required by the college I attended.

My friend Jim Bob owned a sweet 1961 Ford Thunderbird and a beat up 1940's truck of indiscriminate model. He'd chopped everything but the windshield off the cab top with a welding torch, making what we called an instant hillbilly convertible. We'd drive that thing to Tablerock Lake and watch the girls in bikinis play. Lovely, giggly girly visions.

Jim Bob asked, "Would ja' like to take a spin down to Harrison County, Arkansas?" Being a young man of sound mind, I agreed. Sure didn't want to hang around on campus for the weekend. Figured the girls down there were lovely, too.

Jim Bob seemed a little shifty-like when he picked me up. Then, Jim Bob was always kinda shifty-like. He told me the pickup truck was from loving a woman five years older than he, with a three-year old child. He said something about an ex-husband and something about high school romance in the hill country. Anyway, I the ever gullible believed him, that we were headed for an innocent adventure.

We set out south, listening to Wolfman Jack out of Chicago on a patched-in radio from an old Chrysler push button car. We each had a cold beverage from the cooler in the pickup bed amongst the rubble. Sure was easy to reach out into the bed with no cab. Jim Bob did a clever thing. On and on, we flap-rattled south down highway 65 toward Harrison. Top speed 45-miles per hour.

I laughed and talked with the ever shifty Jim Bob, as we turned on a country road in the middle of the Ozarks boondocks. It was an unlighted, rocky, bumpy ride in a wild and dark forest. Up and down hollers we merrily went.

Jim Bob stopped at a road that went straight up to some dark cloud bank somewhere in front of a rusty, locked gate. Owls are hooted and it got curioser and spookier out there. It was 11.30 p.m. and the rest of the God fearing, smart hill folks were abed. Jim Bob fished a key out of his over-all pocket and opened the ramshackle gate. He waved at me. I crammed the rattle trap pickup into first gear and drove through. He re-locked the gate. I slid over and Jim Bob re-entered the driver side. He let out the clutch and started up the hillside in low gear. The truck groaned. He gave me one of those shifty side long glances and looked like he swallered a hoppy toad.

Directly, we came off the ridge top into a

holler. There stood the biggest, meanest, ugliest bib over alled hillbilly I ever did see. The guy peered at me like I was a rodent and he was a hooty owl looking at supper. "What cha brung here, Jim Bob" he sed. He waved an antique twelve gauge shotgun at me. I tried very hard to slide off the seat into the floor boards.

Jim Bob said, "Ken's okay," and hauled me out of the pickup and put my precious soul and body under a big rustling oak.

The man aimed the enormous holes in the double-barrel of a twelve gauge at me. Big Earl didn't care for strangers. My saving grace was I was young and unsophisticated and Big Earl knew that on some level. He sed, "I knowed yo'uns but I cain't say thet about him!" as he pointed me to a seat under the oak.

Jim Bob drove off up the holler and left me under the oak tree with Big Earl. I sweating profuse although the night air was chilly. The huge man practiced spitting his chaw on my pristine white "I Spy" tennie babes – my stylish shoes. I tried not to wince or flinch and kept two very wide eyes on that twelve gauge bore with the twin tunnels aimed in my general direction. It was a harrowing forty five minutes being entertained by a glowering silent giant who spit chaw and grunted monosyllabically.

I put out a hand to rise as Jim Bob came rattlin' back down the holler. Big Earl gestured with the shot gun for me to glue myself in place. I did this without complaint!

Jim Bob grinned at us and escorted me back to the old pickup. He waved nonchalantly at Big Earl and headed back down the huge ridge. Big Earl spat in the general direction of the truck. I remained speechless and shaky until we started back toward Branson on paved highway.

"What was that all about?" I finally squeaked out, with a dry mouth. I still can visualize the twin tunnels of that twelve gauge. I help myself to three or more beverages from the cooler. Jim Bob then informed me he had a stainless steel tank under the junk in his pick up bed. It is now empty of the moonshine he delivered to the holler. I tried hard not to envision prison for aiding and abetting.

"Jim Bob laughed so hard he could barely drive. "I had to drop a load of 'shine off to Big Earl's cuzzins." He howled at my discomfort. "It's dry over thar in Harrison and you know that just ain't right." He howled louder and slapped his thigh, showing his twisted sense of humor.

I guzzled my beverage and tried to practice a little of the Psychology 105 stuff. Tried to forget Big Earl and not kill Jim Bob. At least not while he was driving.

I only twitched for three months every time I saw Jim Bob and that pickup truck after that night. I found out there was a still or two in that holler and revenuers were known to have vanished from memory forever there. Times being what they were. Jim Bob would make another run. He invited me along. Unfortunately, just before our trip, a rival clan of 'shiners had blown up Big Earl's cousin's still.

Whenever Jim Bob invited me to go to the lake

after that, I quizzed him with Treasury agent interrogation techniques. Once, when he didn't give me satisfactory answers, I jumped out of his pickup going north up Highway 65. Didn't take me very long at all to heal up.

About the Author

Kenneth H. Williams holds a Bachelor of Arts in Art Education, and Missouri Lifetime K-12 Teaching Certification. He writes poetry, skits, short stories, and is revising three book length fiction projects. His passions are family, grandchildren, teaching, writing, travel and life. Ken is a decorated veteran with a Bronze Star, Purple Heart and Combat Infantry Badge as well as Army Commendation medal. His poetry is published in The Ozarks Mountaineer, the Journal of the Ozarks, the St. James Leader Journal, and has won several haiku contests at poetry.com.

VIETNAM

Ken Williams, Artist

1969 Welcome Mat

The Scarred Poet

Birds and screeching animals gone silent,
Bamboo rattles in the wind,
The triple canopy jungle looms violent.
Tension mounts as we check the ammo clip,
And step on the welcome mat trail,
And through we try to quietly slip.
Hyper-alert for sounds and booby traps,
Peering thru' the rare openings,
Across the Ho Chi Minh trail according to the maps.
Hunting black clad figures that hunt us,
Planning another Tet offensive,
All careening out of control on war's express bus.
Tensions mount as we hunt men,
And they hunt foreign invaders,
Maligned by public and anchormen,
We just did the job assigned,
And returned to an ungrateful welcome.
Found our country uncaring and unkind.
But here and now we clash,
Kill, fight and mostly win,
Because we learned how to shoot and smash.

The jungle welcome mat is treacherous and deadly,
Adrenaline, fear and cordite scent the battle air,
M79, M60 and M16's play a final medley.
And we stack bodies,
For the all important count,
Vietnam vacation and the endless parties.

About the Author-Artist

The Scarred Poet, aka Kenneth H. Williams, holds a Bachelor of Arts in Art Education, and Missouri Lifetime K-12 Teaching Certification. He writes poetry, skits, short stories, and is revising three book length fiction projects. His passions are family, grandchildren, teaching, writing, travel and life. Ken is a decorated veteran with a Bronze Star, Purple Heart and Combat Infantry Badge as well as Army Commendation medal. His poetry is published in The Ozarks Mountaineer, the Journal of the Ozarks, the St. James Leader Journal, and has won several haiku contests at poetry.com.

Overrun

Ken Williams

"Sarge, get up!" yelled Scooter! "They hit Dau Tieng, it's been overrun!"

I snapped wide awake. "Any orders?"

"Yeah," Scooter said, "We got to go bail 'em out!

"Shit!" I said, "Where the hell were the Wolfhounds and the Cobra gunships?" I started waking up all the squad I could find.

There ain't nothing spookier than driving a big old magnesium aluminum APC target around in the dark. In a combat zone! Lots of Russian RPG rockets in the enemies hands. Punched holes in our tracks like super-heated acetylene torches. It set off all the ammo and rockets inside. The things burned like a giant flare. But that is another story. I checked my watch, 0200 AM. Why couldn't the little bastards fight in the daytime?

We left two tracks to keep security behind us. The rest lumbered out, went around the corner and out onto the exposed bridge. Immediately small arms fire started plinking off the tracks and the road. Scooter saw movement in a window. The stinking village was built right up to the other end of the bridge. He unlimbered his M-79 grenade launcher.

Scotty said, "Wait, Scooter, this is better!" He pulled a LAWS rocket off the inner wall of the track. He flipped it open, slid the tubes apart and aimed at the muzzle flash in the window. With a bang the rocket screamed toward the window. Flash bang! No more small arms fire. Big smoking hole where the window was. Some gnarled little Vietnamese woman, probably the house owner, stepped out the lower door. She was berating us in high pitched Vietnamese. The men on lead track were waving her back in. She didn't get it, until they fired a burst over her head. She disappeared.

Coming up to the Dau Tieng base camp gate, it looked untouched. Two shadowy figures stood up. Close!

"What the hell you doin'!" said someone up front. "I almost shot your ass!"

"Thank God, you guys are here!" The VC are blowing up everything in there." the MP guard said. "There are only two of us, we couldn't do anything. We called it in!"

"Open the damn gate!" growled the platoon sergeant, "let's go send these gooks to their ancestors!"

There was smoke and fires burning, exploded Huey choppers and flaming aircraft blown apart. The POL dump was burning with clouds of oily black smoke. Rounds were pooping off at the smoldering ammo dump. Smoke and CS gas drifted across the runway. People were screaming and moaning. It was like coming into hell. We hopped off the tracks and began or movement forward. We had to crisscross the open runway. The VC were running between building and bunkers. We were taking them out as we advanced. Mostly they were running from us. A few turned to fight but we made short work of that. We spread out moving through Dau Tieng base camp. Slow scary shit. Hunting in the dark, between in every building. Checking bunkers clearing the inside. Body count was going up, but most were dead GIs we found. Freakin' body count that is what the HQ desk riders wanted, to show we were winning. Dead is dead no winning for anyone!

I dashed across the runway near the north eastern edge of the berm. A figure rose before me. I almost squeezed off a burst.

"Chu Hoi!" it croaked. He thought I was a VC! The man reached for me...

No fucking hand! Blown off, to the mid-forearm, bones jutting out and blood squirting.

'Easy, I'm a G.I." I laid him down; I turned and flagged a solider running by. 'Get the medic over here! Now!" I pulled his belt off and cinched down his arm. I handed him the end. "Hold this, Okay?" I popped a morphine vial in his leg.

He started crying, "My buddy is over there!" He motioned with his head.

I saw three other troops, behind me, hiding in the ditch. "Get your ass up and find the fucking medic!"

"I ain't goin' in there, its dark!" one yelled at

me."Gooks running all over!"

"You go find him or I'll shoot you!" I turned my rifle on him. He scurried out of the ditch and between the bunkers.

I moved toward the area indicated by the wounded man. There he lay, gasping in pain. His guts lay over his legs and in the dirty water flowing in the ditch. "Help!" he moaned.

I almost threw up. "Goddamn", I was the only one here. No medic! "Easy, easy friend!" I pulled out his med pack and mine. I cut open his shirt to see. Bloody guts spilled all over, all dirty and strung out. 'Shit!" I began to herd them back up into his sliced open belly. I stopped once to throw up acid bile. I finally got them back up; sort of in. They slid and slipped like live serpents. I held then up with one hand, while stringing bandages over them with the other. I pulled off his shirt and tied the arms together to help hold his intestines in. I wiped my hands on my fatigues. "Shit!" Another damn smell I would never forget. Then I saw our medic coming. I rattled off what I had done. The medic had an armed grunt with him. He was a contentious objector and carried no weapon. "I'm going." I said and headed off numbly.

I stepped into the doorway of the engineers' bunker. Somehow the sun had risen while I was busy.

On the floor was engineer's bodies. One had his face half blown away from a direct RPG hit. One had his dick cut off and shoved into his own mouth. Two had been decapitated and their heads shoved into their sliced open stomachs. Three more were lying cut up and shot dead. Bamboo stakes were driven into the eyes of one. Another had bamboo shoved up his ass. What the fuck kind of war was this? Hate was boiling inside of me. I just wanted to kill something.

I stumbled out to the left, to the Wolfhound bunker on the other side of the runway. An exact duplicate of the scene was inside there. I fell out the door and threw up the nothing in my stomach. Why couldn't I feel anything? Dead! I was dead and mutilated as these corpses. This place had killed something inside of me. I stood shakily and looked out over the berm, at the razor wire in front of the air strip. There were bodies lying everywhere. Looked like some villagers were forced to die to make bridges over the wire. The VC had run over their backs right up the berm, and into the base camp. These people caught between VC and GI and all they wanted to live and grow rice.

Heading back to the tracks (APCs) I saw our platoon 60 caliber machine gunner. "God I love this shit! I can kill and no one gives a crap!" He excitedly told me how he had almost chopped two VC in half with is machine gun. "God, I love it!"

I stood and stared at him. "What?"

Tell me you don't love the killing? It's a fucking rush!" he said.

"Go to hell!" I said as I walked away. I briefly wondered, was he insane or was I? It just don't matter. I couldn't feel anymore. And it was only June. Five more months of this shit!

Author's note:

The two wounded GIs both survived.

About the Author

Kenneth H. Williams, aka The Scarred Poet, holds a Bachelor of Arts in Art Education, and Missouri Lifetime K-12 Teaching Certification. He writes poetry, skits, short stories, and is revising three book length fiction projects. His passions are family, grandchildren, teaching, writing, travel and life. Ken is a decorated veteran with a Bronze Star, Purple Heart and Combat Infantry Badge as well as Army Commendation medal. His poetry is published in The Ozarks Mountaineer, the Journal of the Ozarks, the St. James Leader Journal, and has won several haiku contests at poetry.com.

HUMOR AND NOSTALGIA

Internet Romance

Charles King

Norvell Fillups and his old fishing buddy, I.L. Steel, were sitting in the outside snack area of the Pik-It-Quik convenience store finishing their breakfast. Norvell tilted his chair back on two legs, stretched, then turned up the lukewarm can of RC and drained the last few drops. He scratched his belly beneath his overalls, belched, and set the chair back down on four legs again. He had just had a couple of pickled eggs, an RC, and a half-dozen little chocolate-covered doughnuts. I.L, who was always trying to lose weight, was just sipping on a quart of Gatorade and smoking a cigar.

"Shore is great to finally be sixty two years old, ain't it?" Norvell said, scraping a piece of chocolate off of his false teeth with the flip tab from the RC can.

"Yep, been living all my life fer this day." I.L. answered. "Forty years down at Tannit and Cannit. Honestly, there were some days I thought I wouldn't make it through deer season, working non-stop twelve to fourteen hours a day from Fall right up till the first of the year, processing them Bambis." Then having to get by cutting a little wood and drawing my unemployment until next deer season."

"You's lucky to have a good job like that," Norvell replied. I had that motorcycle wreck when I was nineteen, never was able to do much after that on account of my back."

I.L. nodded in agreement. "Mighty fortunate fer you, Irene had a good job down at the chicken processing plant. That got you through some rough years."

Norvell pushed his hat back, removed a big red bandanna from his back pocket, wiped his balding head and then dabbed at his eyes. "Don't like to think about Irene. Every time I hear her name I think about that no account Horace "Hossmeat" Jones she run off with. Him with his gold tooth and them Lizard cowboy boots and them tall tales about life on the open road. Swept that poor woman off her feet, took her away from me and the good life."

Norvell looked like he might cry. "One minute she was a happy, Barry County housewife, skinning them chickens and providing fer her crippled husband, the next minute she was living a life of sin and debauchery in that big, red Peterbilt with ole Hossmeat, heading fer California with a load of them same chickens she'd been skinning."

"When was it she took off?"

"Be nine years come August. Seems like yesterday," Norvell replied, blowing his nose, then wiping his eyes again before stowing the bandanna in his pocket once more. "I sorta figured once I turned sixty two and started drawing that government check she might decide to come back home."

I.L. looked at Norvell and grinned. "I been hearing you wouldn't let her come back now even if she wanted to."

"Where'd you hear that?"

"Common knowledge around town is that you're seeing somebody. Opal Clambutt up at Walmart said you's in the other day and bought a new pair of overalls and a big bottle of Aqua Velva. Opal can get the news out faster than the newspaper."

I.L. dug in his pocket and come out with a match. He fired it with his thumbnail and re-lit his dead cigar, then took a couple of big puffs. "Word is you been doing some Internet dating." I.L. leaned over close to Norvell and said in a low voice, "You really got one of them computers, Norvell?"

Norvell looked all around to make sure no one was watching, then slipped his hand into the bib pocket of his overalls and pulled out a new smart phone. "What do you think of this gadget?"

I.L.'s eyes lit up. "Show me how it works."

"There's nothing to it. The gal up at Walmart, where I bought it, showed me how to use it. I was a texting like a pro in no time at all," Norvell said, firing up the tiny phone and going to the Internet. "First day I had it I found this place where you can meet these nice, lonely women. It's one of them websites called HotToTrot.com. They's hundreds of lonesome women there just looking fer mature, eligible males like me."

"Tell me about your girl friend you met on there," I.L. said excitedly, breathing a little harder.

I'll do better than that. I'll show you her picture," Norvell said, pushing a couple of buttons and bringing a photo onto the tiny screen."

"My gosh, Norvell, that gal can't be no more than…"

"Twenty six years old," Norvell replied proudly. "She lives in Palm Springs, California, and her Daddy owns a chain of liquor stores out there. She's a part-time swimsuit model."

"What's her name?"

"Good Lord, I.L., don't you know anything about the Internet? Ain't you ever heard of identity theft? She can't use her real name on the Internet on account of someone might steal it."

"What's her Internet name then?"

"Midnight Mamma. That's because she has to work the late shift in her Daddy's liquor store sometimes."

"What's your Internet name, Norvell?"

Norvell dropped his head, blushed, cleared his throat ,then mumbled, "Tennessee Stud."

"Tennessee Stud…why you ain't never even been to Tennessee," I.L. roared, laughing.

"Well," Norvell began meekly, "I might have said I live in Nashville and I used to play guitar fer Sara Evans, in her band, and I might have said I had to quit and move to Arkansas cause Sara got kind of sweet on me."

"Good Lord, Norvell, you're 62 years old. Anybody knows Sara Evans wouldn't have a 62 year old guitar player."

"I might have told her I was twenty six too," Norvell mumbled.

"When are you going to meet her in person?" I.L. asked.

"I'm beginning to think I might just forget about the whole deal," Norvell said, with a sad look on his face. "I know it would break her heart, and I'd probably lose my last chance for happiness, and die a lonesome old bachelor, but I can't figure out a way to meet her."

"I got to thinking, even if I dye my hair and wear sunglasses, she is gonna realize I ain't twenty six years old when she sees me. Then, if she overlooks a little lie about my age, what am I gonna do if she whips out a guitar and wants me to play something like *Wildwood Flower?*"

I.L took a big drag on his cigar and blew a smoke ring. "Shore looks like you painted yourself into a corner. What you gonna do?"

"I ain't decided yet. We're still dickering about where we're going to meet the first time; the Holiday Inn in Albuquerque, New Mexico, or the city park in Pea Ridge, Arkansas. She said she figured Albuquerque was about half way."

"I reckon Pea Ridge was your idea?"

"It was the only town I could think of. I get pretty excited when I'm chatting with Midnight Mamma," Norvell said. "But the dangdest thing, she seemed tickled to death when I mentioned Pea Ridge."

_ A Few Days Later_

Norvell pulls his truck into the Keepit Kleen self-service car wash and finds I.L. checking all the machines for loose change. He rolls down the window and hollers at I.L.

"How's it going?"

"Not too bad. I found two quarters on the ground over by the vacuum cleaner and thirty five cents and a half a pack of Camels somebody left in one of the bays," I.L. replied, walking up to Norvell's truck, lighting a camel with a kitchen match. "How you doing?"

"Doing great, doing great," Norvell answered, grinning like a mule eating briars. "In fact, I'm doing so good I may have a surprise announcement for you one day soon."

"Did you ever decide what to do about meeting your Internet girlfriend?"

"Shore did, in fact we decided to meet in person last Wednesday afternoon at the city park in Pea Ridge."

"Did she turn out to be blind?" I.L. asked, with a quizzical look.

"No, no, she's got the purtiest blue eyes you ever saw. Why would you ask a question like that?"

"I figured she would be expecting to see a good looking, twenty six year old guitar picker. You can't hardly play a radio and them shoes you're wearing are older than twenty six, not to mention the fact you're fat, half bald, and have false teeth."

"Oh that," Norvell grinned. "Turned out Ruby Mae didn't mind. She had fibbed a little, too."

"Ruby Mae?"

"Yup, Ruby Mae Scroggins, that's Midnight Mamma's real name, and turns out she don't live in California either. In fact, she's got a trailer about four miles in the country outside of Pea Ridge. That picture was forty years old. She's sixty three and pushing two hundred pounds, but them things don't matter much to me. She's got a good heart, loves to fish and has a nearly new half- ton Ford truck and an aluminum fishing boat. Reckon my sixties may turn out to be the beginning of the happiest time of my life, thanks to the Internet."

About the Author

Charles King is a third generation native of Barry County, Missouri, and now resides in Springfield. He has had numerous newspaper and magazine articles published and is the author of the humorous novel *The Spiritual Awakening of Earl Eugene Needmore* published through Litho Press. Charles can be reached at ckinghelp@att.net

Joshua

Mitch Hale

The brindle and black bull snorted. His red eyes filled with fear and hatred as he was bearing down heading straight for me. A Fifteen hundred pound steam roller, bawled a loud bray, blowing snot from his nose.

"Haa! Haa!" I shouted, not giving an inch of ground. A fifteen-year-old kid and our herd bull engaged in a deadly game of chicken.

I had three rocks in my hands. The ground trembled under the hooves of the lead bull and twenty head of the thunderous herd rapidly approaching. I threw the three fist sized stones in quick succession, two found their mark. Smack! Pow! The first rock hit old brindle right between the eyes. The second stone caught him on the nose.

I laughed a loud breathless laugh. Bull's-eye! I guess old brindle didn't know I was the starting varsity baseball pitcher.

In an instant he veered to the right, the herd following behind him, heading for the creek. We still had a chance to head them off. My dad's green ford pickup rocketed past me bouncing over the small ditches, pot holes, and clumps of fescue grass, on the eighty acres of prairie we called home near Buffalo, Missouri.

Dad didn't believe in horses to gather his cattle, he had me and Joshua and his old pickup, for our almost weekly cattle drive. Dad raced the truck nudging old brindle with the bumper.

I raced toward the creek and saw Joshua pass me on the left. If Dad didn't turn the cattle at the creek, me or Joshua would jump the creek and with the help of the fence, we'd move them back toward the holding pens by the barn. The creek bank was fast approaching. The trickle of live water was not over three foot wide in the summer but currently in April with the past rains could widen to twenty feet. Dad's truck skidded to a stop by the creek bank scattering dirt and grass into the fast moving current. The cattle turned back and splashed into the creek.

I was running full throttle readying myself for the jump. Joshua was ahead of me but suddenly pulled up short and stopped much as Dad's truck had just done. I saw Joshua eyeing the water as I launched myself off the creek bank mimicking my record breaking long jump, my Junior year in track.

"O, Crap!" The creek was wider than I thought. I came up three feet short of the opposite bank.

"Kersplash!" I landed thigh high in the fast moving creek water, stumbling and falling in the cold churning brine. Soaked from head to toe, I regained my balance, staggering out of the creek. Instantly, I was back to full speed and raced toward my ally, the cross fence. I would beat old brindle and the herd and turn them back toward the corral. My Saturday morning swim had cost me precious seconds as old brindle out ran me to the gate,.

The herd split and dad yelled, "Let's take them another circle."

The green truck forded the creek at a narrow stretch and Dad picked me up. "Mitch, you're soaked, ride in the back. I told you not to throw rocks at our cattle. Joshua. Get up front with me." Joshua, dry as a bone snickered, showing me a full set of pearly white teeth as he jumped into the front seat by Dad, who was planning our next attack on old brindle and the herd.

I said through the back window, "Thanks for the help, Joshua, you jerk."

Joshua peeked to see if Dad was watching as he stuck his tongue out at me, Then curtly turned his back on me.

"Don't worry, Joshua, we'll get them next time." Dad soothed.

I was really beginning to dislike Joshua, Dad's new buddy.

The next few years flew by. I graduated high school leaving dear old Buffalo High School as the school record holder in the mile and two mile run. Cross country running was my specialty.

Reminiscing, I realized all the on-foot cattle drives contributed to my success. I finished college, bought into the family wholesale business, married, and settled down to start a family. By this time Joshua and Dad were inseparable. When I married and moved out, Joshua moved to dad's house. He went to the café each morning and rode with Dad where ever they went. Our import wholesale business grew and my work load increased as multitudes of customers came to our little southern Missouri town to buy our products. Joshua hung out in Dad's office and grew increasingly arrogant and obnoxious.

Joshua didn't help us at all in the business except to create havoc. I can still see him strutting through our warehouse, brown shoulders pushed back narrowed into thin hips and analyzing everything we did. His brown eyes looked right through you. His dark bushy eyebrows matched his blackish blue hair. His belligerent manner, slender build, and stubborn persona, alienated everyone but Dad. I realized my dad had truly adopted Joshua and probably loved him more than me, his third son.

My dad was a huge intimidating man. An old school, gruff, man that grew up poor and was hard to get to know. How had inconsiderate, obtuse Joshua worked his way into my dad's heart? Joshua was deathly scared of storms. I entered Dad's office as thunder roared and lightning flashed and the rain came down like you were pouring it out of a boot.

"Where's Joshua?" I questioned.

Dad nodded at the couch.

Joshua, quivering and shivering was whimpering, hiding behind the divan.

Dad lost control of Joshua as they both got older. Joshua wouldn't listen and would run away and hide around the warehouse as Dad fumed in his office, yelling, "Joshua, come here."

What an unruly, ungrateful fellow!

My relationship with Joshua exploded one day when I walked in my office with a customer and caught Joshua urinating on my desk and paperwork.

I shouted, "Joshua, get out!" I kicked him in the stomach as he jumped trying to grab my throat. I sent a punch to his neck. I'd been waiting for this day.

Joshua snarled, kicking at me, he turned and retreated to Dad's office.

I stormed into the room. "Dad, Joshua pissed on my desk. He's got to go."

Dad and his customer, C. L. Connely, cracked up laughing.

"Joshua, why did you do that?" Dad asked.

Joshua grinned, sticking his tongue out at me.

I snapped. "This is crazy. You've got to get control of him." I stormed out of the room,

Laughter following me.

The next day, Joshua swaggered through the warehouse.

I snickered, "I know you've been in a lot of trouble but Dad has lost his mind."

Joshua frowned, shaking his head. Around his neck, he displayed a primitive looking collar with a beeping, red light. I knew that Dad's cousin, Terry, had used this device when he was sheriff of the county. The device was controlled by a remote that Dad possessed. It sent electrical shock waves to whoever wore the collar.

I heard dad's distant yell, "Joshua, Joshua!"

I turned as my little black haired, brown eyed advisory hugged against me.

"ZZZT-ZZZZT!" The electrical current raced through us both taking us to our knees. Joshua looked skyward as through a bolt of lightning had hit him. He raced to Dad's office.

I felt sick to my stomach. I looked at the crotch of my pants where a dark wet spot had appeared. Joshua had outsmarted me again.

We heard sirens one morning and found Dad's pickup turned over in the same creek we had ran through with old brindle. Joshua was standing guard helping to keep Dad's head out of the cold , spring water.

My dad entered a battle with diabetes and congestive heart failure that he couldn't win.

I did my part keeping the business going and helping when I could. Joshua never left dad's side. When Dad died, it devastated us all but broke Joshua's heart and spirit. Joshua didn't come to the funeral but sat in Dad's truck like a faithful sentinel as everyone drove by headed to the gravesite, most waving or nodding their sympathy to Joshua.

The days following the funeral, Joshua lost any desire to do anything. He lay around the house, not talking to anyone but only mumbling and growling replies that no one could understand.

One day, I drove to Mom's house finding Joshua and Dads friend C. L. Conelly, sitting in the front yard by Dad's truck.

Joshua was howling a mournful cry .

Tears streaming down his cheeks, Connely cried, too. "Bob, what will we do without you? Why did you have to leave us?"

My Mom called me, worry and concern, in her

voice. "Joshua is gone. I haven't seen him in a couple of days since the big thunder storm.

I put on my rubber boots and searched the barn and rolling hills of the eighty acre homestead where Joshua and I had headed cattle years ago. I found Joshua, dead, tangled in a barb wire fence near the swollen creek. He had either been struck by the lightning he so feared or died of a broken heart.

We buried Joshua the next day with an informal ceremony of our family.

I paid my last respects. "Joshua. I know we had our differences but I still admire you. You earned my dad's love and trust. That was difficult for anyone to do. You were his best friend and companion. His life was happier, his illness was made easier, by you being there. Even though you were just a blue healer, stock dog, you made his life and world a better place. "I love you but I'm not going to miss you."

About the Author

Robert Mitchell Hale lives in Buffalo, MO. He graduated from the University of Missouri in Columbia in 1980 with a bachelor's degree in Animal Science. Mitch is an owner of Hale Fireworks, L.L.C., a wholesale business of over 800 customers and 400 family operated retail locations and other businesses. He has three children, Nick, Chayla, and A. J. Mitch's hobby of writing was inspired by his mother, Jane, showing him a different world of imagination and intrigue. They enjoy friendly competition when writing for contests. Mitch's first published work was, "The Business of being a Father", in "Every Day's Is Father's Day", 2006. His short stories, "Checkmate", and "GPS" are published in Mysteries of the Ozarks, Vol. III. and Vol. IV, 2011. "Double Dare YA" was published in 2012. "The White Wolf" will be published in The Best of Frontier Tales in 2015.

On the Road at 69

Ken Williams

69 is a good number,
As roll on miles without slumber,
The reflexes not keen,
Cause you know, no longer a teen.
Hair mostly gone, vision slower,
Traffic impatient; you an unwanted stroller,
Speed limits suggestions, not law,
Road work slows cars and semis to a crawl.
Young men in big pickups ride your tail,
Wanting to go, push you off to a side rail.
But all is not a pain,
Cause stations and drive thru's love you,
Having disposable income is not in vain.
Miles roll by in endless streams,
Until the vastness becomes dreams.
Miles and miles of miles,
Makes you lust for motels with smiles.
Continental breakfast a euphemism for calories,
Seeking cash for sleep, host mentalities.
Destination lost in the journeys,
Passing and re-passing the turkeys.

When the end is near.
Seeing family so dear.
Time slipping quickly by,
As you repack with a sigh.
On the road again,
As unfolding vistas will begin.
Never the destination,
Always the journey's evocation.
On the road again,
New and old scenes begin.

About the Author

Kenneth H. Williams holds a Bachelor of Arts in Art Education, and Missouri Lifetime K-12 Teaching Certification. He writes poetry, skits, short stories, and is revising three book length fiction projects. His passions are family, grandchildren, teaching, writing, travel and life. Ken is a decorated veteran with a Bronze Star, Purple Heart and Combat Infantry Badge as well as Army Commendation medal. His poetry is published in The Ozarks Mountaineer, the Journal of the Ozarks, the St. James Leader Journal, and has won several haiku contests at poetry.com.

SPECULATIVE FICTION

Tall True Tales?

Jane Hale

I used to listen to my dad and his friends talk about their experiences. I heard some pretty tall tales. But, the strangest tall tale I can remember hearing was from a man we visited near Marshfield, Missouri back in the sixties. During the evening the man shared this tall tale. He claims it is true. You draw your own conclusion.

Tom's True Tale

"I awoke with the vividness of my dream still with me. I was drifting, pushing my way through mists of fog. Drafts of cold air swirled about me, my footsteps echoed back through the inky blackness of the night. Where was I?

Like a fist in the gut, reality hit me. I was not safely asleep on a homeward bound train to Marshfield, Missouri. I was walking calmly along a deserted railroad track in the dark of night. I had no idea where on God's earth I was. My mind searched for answers.

Yesterday, my brother, Jed, his blue heeler, Oscar, and I, herded our cattle to Conway to load on the train for market. The cattle had been jumpy and the ride to Saint Louis, Missouri was stifling. The yards were busy. Everyone was selling and prices were low. In short, everything went wrong.

As we boarded the old freight out of Saint Louis headed for Springfield, Missouri we agreed it would be a blessing to get home. Shifting our butts on the hard seats of the back car, we tried to get easy. The few passengers ahead of us were asleep. Oscar dozed beneath the seat. A slight breeze drifted in the open window, soon Jed and I were sawing logs, too. Then - -

I forced my feet to stop and stared about me in wonder. "What in the hell are you doing out here, Tom, boy?"

My voice echoed back through the fog asking me the same question. For the first time in my life Tom didn't have an answer. I could have set down right there on those tracks and bawled if I thought it would help. I knew in my heart it wouldn't. Instead, I found myself chuckling when I tried to imagine the expression on Jed's face when he awoke and found me gone.

"Oscar, where's Tom? What kind of a watch dog are you?"

I knew if it was Jed out here on the tracks Oscar would be right beside him. Blue Heelers are good dogs and true to their master.

Then the seriousness of my situation hit me. I knew I must make a decision. Would I follow the railroad track or cut out cross-country?

I'll never know what I might of done because a small miracle happened. I was due one. A slow moving light on my right informed me there was a highway not too far away. Thank God I hadn't removed my boots when I went to sleep. Stumbling, sliding, I started down the steep chat embankment and hit out for the highway.

The road took me to a small town. In the early morning light I located the depot. I questioned the old man at the desk."When's the next train to Springfield? I need to be on it."

"Train passed through not more than a hour ago. You should of been on it." He wallowed a mouthful of tobacco, spit a wad across the room at a spittoon. A perfect hit.

"I was." I mumbled.

"You was - - what?" The old man looked up. A frown line creased his brow.

"On it," I said , searching my pockets for money to buy a ticket home. I found only small change. Not nearly enough to buy me a ticket. I knew I needed a friend.

The old man smiled, withdrew a tobacco pouch, and offered me a chew. "Care to have a seat and tell me your tale?"

It was clear if I wanted help from this old man, I would have to tell him the whole story or what I knew of it.

He settled back with an amused expression on his face that spoke louder than words. I've heard them all son.

My grin had a vocabulary, too. I bet you've never heard one like this Pop. And . . . I began my story."

Tom chuckled. "To this day, I don't know how I got off that train, I've told my story to a lot of people. Some believe it, others don't. Don't make me no never mind whether they do or don't. You folks, believe it if you want to, if you don't just chalk it up to a tall tale."

I tended to believe Tom. Why would he tell a story like that if it wasn't true? I've thought about his story lots of times especially when I'm driving along the highway on a foggy night. Times like that I can almost imagine old Tom stumbling alone lost in the night.

And, how about you? What do you think?

About the Author

Jane Shewmaker Hale resides on the Hale family farm in Buffalo, Missouri and is an active partner in all family businesses. She is a charter member Ozark Writer's; member of the Springfield

Writer's Guild, the Ozark Writers League, and the Missouri Writers' Guild. Writing consists of a weekly column, "Buffalo...As I Remember it" in the County Courier since 1993, a series of YA mysteries: Wonderland 1997, Heartland 1999, Foreverland 2001, and Boomland, 2003. Mollycoddles, a collection of plush animals are book companions. Every Day Is Mother's Day 2003, Every Day Is Father's Day 2006. "Lucky Stiff," "Beg, Borrow, and Steal" "The Wish" and "Boo! Who?" are short stories published in the Ozark Writers Inc. Mystery Anthology series, Vol. I, II, III., and IV. Her short story, "Bye and Bye," won the online contest on Frontier Tales and will be published in 2014.

Carlene's Diary: Time Travel?

Marilyn Smith

"Battered, Bruised, and Left for Dead," headline in the June 8, 1961 *Springfield Leader-Press* caught my attention as I searched for blog topics.

"A young girl was found by Anthony Saunders, in a wooded area between Northview and Strafford, along Highway 66. It is believed Saunders suffers from a mental illness, rendering him incapable of relating the details of the early morning incident," the newspaper coverage began. "Saunders claims to be a graduate of Kickapoo High School, in Springfield, a nonexistent institution. He even produced a fake Missouri driver's license showing his birth date as December 14, 1994."

Although I generally steer clear

of crime stories, my curiosity pushed me onward.

"Central High student, Carlene Keller, 15, is still in critical condition, at Burge Hospital, following an attempt yesterday to end her life," the June 9 coverage stated. "Had it not been for Anthony Saunders, who stopped along Highway 66, east of Strafford, to check the thump, thump, thump of a tire, she might not have been found before she succumbed to her injuries. No further details were available."

Time travel? Impossible, I thought. Surprisingly, with the help of an Internet search site, I tracked Anthony. Although reluctant to tell his story, he agreed, with the stipulation I change all names and dates to protect the identities of those involved. The following is his account:

On a day free from classes in Rolla, he decided to visit his friends and family in Springfield. When he approached the off-ramp at Northview, something told him to take that route. After traveling only a few miles beyond the turnoff, he suspected tire trouble and stopped. While inspecting the tires he noticed an old suitcase in the ditch, and with visions of drug money being thrown from a plane, he retrieved it. A deserted road stretched before him as he popped the trunk and heaved the muddy suitcase up and into the car's trunk. He broke the latch, then with a bit of reluctance and anticipation he supposed, he raised the lid. The instant it opened, he was nearly blinded by a flash of light. When his eyes refocused, he found himself standing on a much narrower road, his new Ford Taurus was gone and in its place was a green Chevrolet, with 1961 license plates. The suitcase appeared to be new, also. Packed tightly inside, he found women's clothing. Underneath was a pink diary. Written on the inside cover, "To Carlene, from Grandma Nichols."

Right then an overwhelming urge rushed over him to go back into the woods to see if he could find the owner of the suitcase. Only a few hundred yards beyond where he found the piece of luggage, he saw a young girl on the ground. Not only was she severely beaten, she had red marks on her neck indicating someone had attempted to strangle her.

He reached into his pocket and brought out his cell phone. After punching 9-1-1, he realized those emergency numbers didn't exist in 1961, and he would need to take the girl to the hospital himself.

With a strength he didn't know he possessed, he picked the girl up and carried her to the car. It was a real struggle to get her almost lifeless body into the back seat. "Hold on. I'm going to take you to the hospital," he told her. Her eyes opened a tiny sliver, then she smiled.

The first chance he had at the hospital to go in to see this girl, she asked in an almost inaudible voice something that sounded like "Are you my guardian angel?"

"Your guardian angel? Me, an angel! I'm just

a kid who stopped along the road, at the right time, I guess." Before he had a chance to say another word, Carlene's nurse told him he should not be in there, and shooed him out. "I'll be back to see you," he said.

That afternoon Detective Daniels followed Anthony to his car to retrieve the suitcase. An instant after the car's trunk lid closed, another flash of light occurred. When Anthony's eyes cleared, he was back on Old Route 66. His Ford Taurus was sitting in front of him, and he had to sit down on the pavement to keep from falling.

He thought maybe he had blacked out earlier, and everything about Carlene was some sort of an illusion. The first thing he noticed when he attempted to get up was her diary. It was next to the rear tire. Carlene did exist!

While reading the diary, he learned that she was pregnant, and her mother told her she would not help raise a bastard child. The younger brother, named Leonard, was listed in the phone book as living in Nixa. He said his sister lived in an apartment on Walnut Lawn, near Kansas Expressway.

When Carlene came to the door, the day Anthony visited, it was as if an older version of his mother was standing there. He handed her the diary, and said, "I told you I'd be back later. You just didn't know it would be fifty years later, did you?"

Obviously, from the stunned look on her face, seeing him the same as he looked fifty years ago, even wearing the same clothes, it must have been a shock. "Are you Anthony? The detective said you and the car disappeared into thin air. He looked everywhere for you, but didn't find a trace," Carlene said.

They spent the remainder of the afternoon trying to sort out the details of the events that took place only a couple of days ago, for Anthony, or fifty years ago for her. Due to her injuries, the majority of her memories from that time period were erased.

On the day Anthony found Carlene, back in 1961, she was on her way to meet Jason Blakley, the father of her child. He was due to return to Korea, where he was serving in the Marines. Her next door neighbor offered her a ride, then raped and beat her and left her for dead.

"I'm pretty certain you are my grandmother," Anthony said. "My mother looks so much like you, and she was adopted. Her birthday is December 13, 1961. If you are my grandmother, that would be awesome!" And so it was, as DNA tests revealed.

After introducing his mother to her biological mother, Anthony made an excuse to leave. "They had fifty years of catching up to do, and they didn't need a pesky little grandson interfering." Anthony said.

In the end, I decided not to publish this story in my "Then and Now, All Around Springfield" blog—who would ever believe it?

About the Author

Marilyn K. Smith has written a weekly column for the *Buffalo Reflex Newspaper*, called "A Tale or Two," since 1989. Over 2,000 of her articles have appeared in the *Reflex*, *The Ozarks Mountaineer*, *Springfield! Magazine, Senior Living Newspaper, Ozarks Watch, Springfield News-Leader,* and others. Anthologies her stories are featured in include *Cactus Country Vol. II, Golden Words, Echoes of the Ozarks Vol. VIII, Mysteries of the Ozarks Vol. III, Gifts of the Great Spirit Vol. II.* She serves as a contributing editor of the "Journal of the Ozarks" magazine. Her books include "A History of Highway 65, from the middle of the road," and "The Window Pane Inn and other short stories" published by Litho Press.

ACKNOWLEDGEMENTS

To each of the contributors, I – and the Alzheimer's patients who cannot speak for themselves – extend a heartfelt thank you! Each of you has some connection to a loved one, acquaintance, or caregiver for an Alzheimer's patient and are sympathetic to the mission of this book project – to help raise funds for patients' therapies. Alzheimer's is a dreadful disease, one that claimed my mother's life in June, 2004.

A special thank you goes to Sharon Kizziah-Holmes, owner of Paperback-Press, the publisher of this book. Her skills, creativity, and generous heart make her a much beloved friend and colleague.

Additional thanks to informed reader John R. (Jack) Rayl for advice with the book's organization. As editor, I needed new insights, and appreciate his willingness to assist with that task.

Ann Ragland Bowns is a professional artist and cousin; her offer for me to use any of the incredible creations featured on her web site make this book cover extra special. Thank you, thank you, thank you!

Joyce Ragland

THE ELLA RAGLAND CHARITY

The mission of the Ella Ragland Art 501 (c) (3) company is twofold: (1) to celebrate and remember Ella Ragland as a talented, creative and generous person, not just an Alzheimer's victim; (2) raise funds for Alzheimer's patient therapies.

Ella Ragland was a hobby artist who created more than 200 oil paintings during her early retirement in the 1980s. A highlight of her painting days was when her "Sleepy Trout Fisherman" was selected as a finalist in the Missouri Trout Stamp contest and was displayed in the state capitol.

Mom – Ella developed Alzheimer's and stopped painting. The last two years of her life were spent in a secure ward in a skilled care facility where Alzheimer's patients received special care, but like other facilities I've observed, no therapy that focused on the special needs of Alzheimer's patients. She died in June, 2004.

In 2005, I founded the Ella Ragland Art company as a not-for-profit entity, a charity, in order to raise funds that I could dedicate to Alzheimer's patient therapies. I funded a research project with a certified music therapist and watched him work magic with end stage patients. Next, I created greeting cards and prints made from Mom's oil paintings and sold them at festival booths, online, and in local stores.

Special thanks go to various businesses and

individuals that contribute cash donations each year. The owners of those businesses are long term sponsors of the charity and as such, have helped fund many hours of wonderful palliative care for Alzheimer's patients in Lebanon, Marshfield, Buffalo, and Springfield, Missouri.

Special thanks to sponsors

MacCreed's Art Gallery & Gifts
www.MacCreeds.org

Whimsy Store
www.Whimsy.org

Heaven Scent Bakery www.foursquare.com/v/heaven-scent-bakery

Paperback-Press
www.paperback-press.com

Stiles Roofing of Lebanon, MO

Williams Appraisal

All proceeds from the sale of this book, whether paperback form or e-books, will go to patient projects. We have no overhead for office space, and none of our officers is paid – all donate services.

Please visit our web site
www.EllaRaglandArt.org.

Send comments by email to
EllaRaglandArt@yahoo.com

About the Editor

Joyce Ragland is the daughter of Ella Ragland, whose life and words inspired her to "get out and make something of yourself."